D0474344

MUG MEALS

MUG MEALS

DELICIOUS MICROWAVE RECIPES

DINA CHENEY

JACKSON COUNTY LIBRARY SERVICES
MEDFORD, OREGON 97501

Text © 2015 by Dina Cheney
Photographs © 2015 by Andrew Purcell
All rights reserved.

The Taunton Press, Inc., 63 South Main Street, PO Box 5506, Newtown, CT 06470-5506
e-mail: tp@taunton.com

Editor: Carolyn Mandarano
Copy Editor: Nina Rynd Whitnah
Indexer: Heidi Blough
Jacket/Cover Design: Sandra Salamony
Interior Design: Sandra Salamony
Layout: Sandra Salamony
Photographer: Andrew Purcell
Food Stylist: Carrie Purcell
Prop Stylist: Paige Hicks

The following names/manufacturers appearing in *Mug Meals* are trademarks: Applegate Farms®, Bonne Maman®, Casa Di Bertacchi®, Corn Flakes®, Frontera®, Ghiradelli®, Goya®, Häagen-Dazs®, Heinz®, Horizon® Organic, Kind®, Imagine®, La Famiglia DelGrosso®, Maranatha®, Microplane®, Nature's Path™, Nestle®, Nutella®, Pacific Organic®, Panasonic®, Patsy's®, Rao's Homemade®, Santa Cruz Organic®, Sarabeth's®, Sargento®, Swanson®, Tabatchnick®, Thai® Kitchen, Xochitl™

Library of Congress Cataloging-in-Publication in progress

ISBN: 978-1-62710-916-1

Printed in the United States of America
10 9 8 7 6 5 4 3 2 1

DEDICATION

To my beloved grandmother, Thelma (1927-2014)

ACKNOWLEDGMENTS

Thanks to my kind, thoughtful, and intelligent editor, Carolyn Mandarano, who brought me a project that's truly changed the way I cook. Never again will I look at a microwave the same way! It's been a joy and a creative challenge to play around with the ingredients in my pantry. It's also been liberating and exciting to experience the instant gratification of turning out delicious dishes in mere minutes. Thanks as well to the rest of the incredible team at The Taunton Press—by now, you've become almost like family! Thank you, thank you to Sandra Salamony and photography team Andrew and Carrie Purcell for the gorgeous design and photographs. Finally, I am so grateful to my husband, Koby, for supporting my career. And Max and Abe, thanks for being my tasters!

INTRODUCTION:
MUG MAGIC!

GRANOLA BARS, THAI curried pumpkin bisque, meatloaf, chocolate espresso pudding, and chocolate truffles—all ready in about 5 minutes? Yes, it *is* possible, thanks to the microwave. This often-overlooked appliance can be used for more than heating up frozen food and melting butter and chocolate. Just combine ingredients from your pantry and freezer in a microwaveable mug, cook in the microwave, and end up with the 125 delicious and satisfying breakfasts, lunches, dinners, and desserts in this book. It sounds simple—and it really is!

In these pages, you'll find dishes that you never thought could possibly come out of a mug—classics like lasagna, meatball Parmesan, and gingerbread, plus surprising twists such as Hawaiian-style fried rice with pineapple, pizza toss, Korean meatballs, and chocolate truffles.

All of these recipes require very little in the way of effort (just a couple of steps) and time (most take a total of 5 minutes). Furthermore, you don't need any cooking skills or even a full kitchen. As long as you have access to a microwave and sink (and single burner in some cases), you're on your way to preparing delicious meals in mere minutes. Whether you're a student (10 or older), are cooking for one or two, or are remodeling your kitchen, this book is for you.

Mug meals are especially convenient in the mornings, when you're in a rush to get out of the house. They're also ideal for after-school snacks, lunches at the office, simple dinners, and treats to satisfy dessert cravings in a flash. For those of you with kids, these recipes might be the first meals they make from scratch.

As you begin to cook from this book, you'll likely find yourself bringing home leftovers from restaurants (like take-out rice) and using up leftovers from your own dinners. You might also begin to keep your pantry stocked, keep chopped onions and peppers in the fridge, and cook off large batches of ground meat and grains, so you're only minutes away from one of the meals and desserts in this book.

These recipes are extremely easy. Still, I wanted to give you some pointers to ensure complete success.

RECIPE POINTERS

■ While most of the dishes in this book are made in a 12-oz. mug, sometimes sauces splatter. For this reason, it never hurts to use a 16-oz. (or larger) mug.

■ It's a smart idea to coat the inside of the mug with cooking spray. The spray will make cleanup easier and allow you to easily invert food out of the mug. That said, I only call for cooking spray if I think it will make a significant difference, as with cakes, chocolate bark, oatmeal, and eggs.

■ Since these dishes rely on just a few ingredients, make sure they're high quality. A dish prepared with watery and bland salsa, for instance, will result in a watery and bland dish. I've listed some of my favorite brands in the sidebar on p. 11.

■ You can mix most ingredients in the mug. However, your food will come out better if you mix the ingredients in a bowl and then pour them into the mug. That said, if in a pinch, know that you *can* do without the bowl, if necessary.

■ It's best to microwave one serving at a time. Microwaving more than one mug will significantly increase the cooking time and throw off the recipe. Since cooking times generally range from 1 to 3 minutes, cooking portions individually isn't too inconvenient, even if you're entertaining. That said, you can probably fit two or three mugs in a standard microwave at the same time; just beware of the outcome.

■ Almost always cover food in the microwave. It will cook more evenly, retain more moisture, and generate less mess. You can use a paper towel or clean kitchen towel, plate or bowl, or piece of waxed paper. Just don't use foil or anything else metallic—metal can catch fire in the microwave.

■ Making mug cakes can be very messy—the batter can easily overflow and get all over the mug and microwave turntable. Like a wacky science experiment, the cakes can pop up out of the mug and later deflate. When this happens, the cover might fall off. Don't worry. Just open the microwave, put the cover back on, and keep microwaving. Use a 16-oz. (or larger) mug when preparing mug cakes.

■ When food comes out of the microwave, it is generally very hot. Always use oven mitts and wait for at least a couple of minutes before eating.

HOW TO USE THIS BOOK

■ As noted, most dishes are prepared in a microwaveable 12-oz. mug on the high setting, though some require a microwaveable 16-oz. mug. Specific size is listed in every recipe.

■ Generally, I use all-purpose flour, kosher salt, large eggs, and granulated (or white) sugar unless I specify otherwise. Since they're easier to find, I use lightly sweetened peanut butter and applesauce. To make dishes healthier, feel free to swap in sugar-free peanut butter and applesauce and low- or no-sodium products, such as broth or canned beans. For those avoiding animal products, substitute rinsed and drained canned beans for cooked meat. Agave nectar can replace honey, and nondairy milk can be substituted for cow's milk. Feel free to substitute frozen for fresh fruits and vegetables, and vice versa. You just might need to adjust cooking times slightly.

■ Some recipes call for cooked meat or grains. Since ground meat usually comes in packages of 1 pound or more and it's handy to have cooked ingredients on hand, I would recommend cooking off more than you need. Keep the cooked ingredients in your fridge (3 or 4 days for meat and up to a week for grains). Then prepare three or four recipes with that ingredient in that week.

■ Several dishes, including several baked goods, can be inverted for serving. To do so, hold a small plate over the top of the mug and flip over, keeping the plate against the rim of the mug with your hand. Gently lift the mug off the baked good. If called for in your recipe, drizzle the cake or muffin with sauce or top with whipped cream or ice cream.

COOKING TECHNIQUES

■ To cook ground meat, heat a sauté pan over medium-high heat and add about 1 teaspoon of vegetable oil. When warm, add the meat to the pan. Cook, stirring with a wooden spoon to break up the meat, until it's opaque and cooked through. Red meat should become brown (rather than pink or red). Poultry should become white rather than pink or beige. It takes about 8 to 10 minutes to cook 1 to 1½ pounds of meat.

■ To boil pasta or rice, fill a medium to large pot two-thirds full of water and salt generously. Cover and bring to a boil over high heat. Once boiling, stir in the grain or pasta and cook, stirring occasionally, until cooked through, following the package instructions for cooking times. For pasta, cook for the minimum amount of time stated on the package since you'll be cooking the dish a bit more in the microwave.

■ You can also use the simmer-steam method to cook rice. Add the rice and twice the amount of water (plus a bit of salt) to a medium to large pot, cover, and bring to a boil over medium-high heat. Once boiling, cover and reduce the heat to low. For white rice, simmer for about 20 minutes, then turn off the heat and let the rice sit and steam for 5 minutes. Fluff with a fork. For brown rice, cook for 35 to 40 minutes; with brown rice, you will likely need to check it and add a bit more water during the cooking process.

■ To cook quinoa, combine the quinoa and twice as much water in a pot with a bit of salt. Bring to a boil over high heat. Once boiling, immediately cover and reduce to a simmer over low to medium-low heat. Cook until the quinoa is tender and the grain has a squiggly shape in the center, 15 to 20 minutes.

MUG MEAL ARSENAL

You need very few tools to prepare the recipes in this book, as noted here.

- A mug—make sure it's microwaveable!
- A small plate
- Microwave (ideally, a 1,100- or 1,200-watt model, such as a Panasonic® NN-SN651B)
- Bowls, at least one small to medium and one small
- Liquid measuring cup
- Measuring spoons
- Spoons
- Forks
- Potato masher
- Box grater
- Microplane® or citrus zester
- Vegetable peeler
- Chef's knife
- Serrated knife (nice to have, but optional)
- Cutting board
- Can opener
- Parchment or waxed paper

RECOMMENDED PANTRY

Here is a list of ingredient staples for mug meals.

SAVORY PANTRY

- Barbecue sauce
- Boxed and canned soups
- Canned beans
- Canned green chiles
- Canned pumpkin and/or squash purée
- Chicken and/or vegetable broth
- Grains: dried pasta, farro, quinoa, quick-cooking oats, rice (brown and white)
- Ketchup
- Low-sodium soy sauce
- Marinara sauce
- Mustard
- Nonstick cooking spray
- Oil
- Pesto
- Plain whole-wheat breadcrumbs
- Salsa
- Spices
- Tomato paste
- Tortilla chips
- Unseasoned rice vinegar

SWEET PANTRY

- All-purpose flour
- Baking powder and baking soda
- Canned coconut milk
- Canned fruit and applesauce
- Chocolate chips
- Dessert sauces
- Dried fruit
- Fruit juice
- Fruit preserves
- Graham crackers and/or graham cracker crumbs
- Granola
- Granulated sugar
- Honey and maple syrup
- Nuts
- Peanut butter (preferably smooth)
- Unsweetened and sweetened shredded coconut

REFRIGERATED SECTION

- Grated cheese
- Hot dogs
- Large eggs
- Milk
- Smoked salmon

FREEZER SECTION

- Frozen breakfast sausage
- Frozen fruits and vegetables
- Frozen meatballs
- Vanilla ice cream

RECOMMENDED BRANDS

Brands listed below are my favorites and all have relatively widespread availability. In some cases, the quality of the product is particularly important; this is noted in individual recipes.

- Broth: Swanson®, Tabatchnick®, Pacific Organic®, Imagine®
- Cheese: Sargento®, Horizon® Organic
- Chocolate chips: Ghiradelli®, Nestle®
- Salsa: Frontera®
- Frozen meatballs: Casa Di Bertacchi®
- Frozen sausage: Applegate Farms®
- Granola: Kind®, Nature's Path™
- Indian curry sauce: Maya Kaimal
- Ketchup: Heinz®
- Marinara sauce: La Famiglia DelGrosso®, Rao's Homemade®, Patsy's®
- Peanut butter: Maranatha®, Santa Cruz Organic®
- Preserves: Sarabeth's®, Bonne Maman®
- Thai curry paste: Thai® Kitchen
- Tortilla chips: Xochitl™
- Vanilla ice cream: Häagen-Dazs®

BREAKFAST

BREAKFAST FARRO WITH BLUEBERRIES

Nourishing and delicious, this breakfast can also serve as a snack or dessert; just add more maple syrup. Feel free to stir in some fresh lemon zest and to substitute other types of fruit for the blueberries and other cooked whole grains for the farro. If you use unthawed frozen fruit, cook the dish for a bit longer; start with another 30 seconds and increase the time if needed to make the farro warm.

- 1 cup cooked farro
- ½ cup milk
- ¼ cup blueberries (fresh or frozen)
- 1 tsp. maple syrup
- ⅛ tsp. kosher salt
- ⅛ tsp. ground cinnamon

1. Stir together the ingredients in a small to medium bowl.

2. Pour into a 12-oz. mug. Cover and microwave until warm, about 1½ minutes.

APRICOT POACHED IN EARL GREY TEA, WITH GRANOLA

Feel free to vary the types of tea and fruit in this healthy breakfast, snack, or dessert—just make sure to use a small piece. To make 6 oz. of Earl Grey tea, let a tea bag sit in 6 oz. of boiling water in the mug for 4 to 5 minutes, then remove and discard the tea bag.

6 oz. hot brewed Earl Grey tea
2 to 3 tsp. honey
1 ripe apricot, halved and pit removed
2 Tbs. granola
Vanilla yogurt, for serving (optional)

1. Add the honey to the brewed tea in the mug and stir well. Add the apricot halves and place a ramekin or small bowl that will fit inside the mug on top to weigh down and cover the fruit.

2. Microwave until the apricot is tender, 1½ to 2 minutes. Transfer the fruit to a small bowl and top with about 1 Tbs. of the poaching liquid and the granola. If desired, top with yogurt.

DOUBLE BERRY FRENCH TOAST

At the bottom of the mug, you'll find a raspberry preserve "surprise."
Feel free to sprinkle with confectioners' (powdered) sugar or
cinnamon sugar (mix together 1 tsp. ground cinnamon with 1 Tbs.
granulated sugar) for an even more decadent breakfast or dessert.
Cinnamon raisin bread or any unflavored country bread would be
delicious substitutes for the croissant, brioche, or challah roll.

Nonstick cooking spray
¼ cup milk
1 large egg
1 Tbs. maple syrup
⅛ tsp. kosher salt
⅛ tsp. ground cinnamon
1 tsp. pure vanilla extract
1 cup 1-inch pieces croissant, brioche, or challah roll
1 Tbs. raspberry preserves
10 fresh berries, such as raspberries, for serving

1. Spray the inside of a 12-oz. mug with cooking spray.

2. Combine the milk, egg, 1 tsp. of the syrup, salt, cinnamon, and
vanilla in a small to medium bowl. Whisk well with a fork. Add the
bread and stir, soaking for 2 minutes.

3. Meanwhile, spoon the preserves into the mug. Place the soaked
bread pieces on top (discard any remaining liquid).

4. Cover and microwave until the liquid mixture solidifies, about
2 minutes (some egg white might be visible). Top with the remaining
syrup and the berries.

GRANOLA BAR WITH APRICOTS, COCONUT, AND CASHEWS

This delicious granola bar is sweet, salty, fruity, and nutty. If you have a nut allergy, substitute pumpkin or sesame seeds for the cashews.

Nonstick cooking spray
2 Tbs. quick-cooking oats
2 Tbs. cooked quinoa
2 Tbs. finely chopped dried apricots (about 6)
1 Tbs. finely chopped cashews
1 Tbs. unsweetened shredded coconut
2 Tbs. vegetable oil
2 Tbs. maple syrup
¼ tsp. kosher salt

1. Spray the inside of a 12-oz. mug with the cooking spray.

2. In a small to medium bowl, stir together all of the ingredients. Pour the mixture into the mug.

3. Cover and microwave until the oats are cooked, about 3 minutes.

4. Pour the hot mixture onto a piece of parchment or waxed paper, shaping into a rectangle or traditional narrow bar. Refrigerate until cold and solid, 30 minutes or more.

EGGS WITH GREEN CHILES AND TORTILLA CHIPS

Try these Tex-Mex eggs served with a warm tortilla, refried beans, sour cream, and guacamole. Mango juice would be ideal alongside.

Nonstick cooking spray
2 large eggs
2 Tbs. frozen corn, thawed and drained
2 Tbs. finely chopped seeded tomato
1 Tbs. shredded Mexican cheese
2 tsp. finely chopped red onions
1 tsp. canned green chiles, drained
⅛ tsp. kosher salt
⅛ tsp. ground coriander
⅛ tsp. ground cumin
4 to 5 tortilla chips
1 tsp. finely chopped fresh cilantro leaves (optional)

1. Spray the inside of a 12-oz. mug with cooking spray.

2. In a small bowl, whisk together the eggs, corn, tomato, cheese, onions, chiles, salt, coriander, and cumin. Pour into the mug.

3. Cover and microwave until the eggs are mostly cooked through, about 1½ minutes. Stir. Re-cover and microwave until cooked through in the center, about another 20 seconds.

4. Crumble chips on top. If desired, sprinkle with cilantro.

LOX AND BAGEL STRATA

To simplify the recipe, you can omit the onions, chives, or zest, but they add a sophisticated "Sunday brunch" flavor. You can also try an onion or challah roll instead of the bagel or, for a healthier dish, opt for a whole-wheat bagel. Feel free to top with a dollop of plain Greek yogurt.

> **Nonstick cooking spray**
> **½ cup milk**
> **1 large egg**
> **1 Tbs. minced fresh chives**
> **1 Tbs. finely chopped red onions**
> **¼ tsp. fresh lemon zest**
> **⅛ tsp. kosher salt**
> **½ "everything" bagel, cut into ½-inch pieces (1 cup)**
> **¼ cup finely chopped smoked salmon**

1. Spray the inside of a 12-oz. mug with cooking spray.

2. Add the milk, egg, chives, onions, zest, and salt to a small to medium bowl and whisk together with a fork. Add the bagel pieces and soak for 5 minutes, pressing down to submerge.

3. Place the bagel pieces in the mug (discard the liquid). Add the salmon and stir well with the fork to spread evenly.

4. Cover and microwave until the center cooks through, about 2½ minutes.

BANANA PEANUT BUTTER OATMEAL

Be sure to use quick-cooking oats for this delicious, high-protein breakfast—my sons' new favorite meal!

½ cup milk
1 mashed very ripe banana (scant ½ cup)
¼ cup quick-cooking oats
1 Tbs. creamy peanut butter
1 tsp. honey
½ tsp. pure vanilla extract
⅛ tsp. kosher salt
⅛ tsp. ground cinnamon

1. Combine all of the ingredients in a small bowl and mix well. Pour into a 12-oz. mug.

2. Cover and microwave until the oats are cooked, about 2 minutes.

• • • • • • • • • • • • • •

APPLE PIE OATMEAL

A much lighter version of apple pie, this warm breakfast just might become a staple at your house. Be sure to use quick-cooking oats.

½ cup milk
½ cup quick-cooking oats
¼ cup plus 2 Tbs. applesauce
2 Tbs. apple juice
¼ tsp. kosher salt
¼ tsp. ground cinnamon

1. Combine all of the ingredients in a small bowl and mix well. Pour into a 12-oz. mug.

2. Cover and microwave until the oats are cooked, about 2 minutes.

EGGS FLORENTINE

This simple version of the classic brunch dish means you don't need a special occasion to enjoy it.

Nonstick cooking spray
1 cup fresh spinach leaves (washed and patted dry), coarsely chopped
¼ cup milk
¼ tsp. plus a pinch of kosher salt
⅛ tsp. ground nutmeg
⅛ tsp. crushed red pepper flakes
1 large egg
1 to 2 slices toasted country bread, such as ciabatta
1 tsp. extra-virgin olive oil

1. Spray the inside of a 12-oz. mug with cooking spray.

2. Stir together the spinach, milk, ¼ tsp. salt, nutmeg, and pepper flakes in a small bowl. Pour into the mug. Crack the egg on top and sprinkle with a pinch of salt.

3. Cover and microwave until the egg is cooked through, 2 to 3 minutes (3 minutes will yield a fully cooked yolk).

4. Transfer the toast to a plate. Carefully remove the spinach-egg mixture from the mug and place on top of the toast (discard the liquid at the bottom of the mug). Drizzle with the oil.

"BAKED" EGG WITH COUNTRY BREAD, SPINACH, AND TOMATO

Full of flavor, this complete meal is even more beautiful garnished with extra diced tomato or finely chopped fresh parsley or basil. For a healthier dish, use whole-wheat country bread and a lower-fat cheese.

> Nonstick cooking spray
> 1 cup fresh spinach leaves, stems removed, washed, and patted
>   dry with paper towels
> 1 cup 1-inch cubes fresh country bread, such as ciabatta
> 3 Tbs. diced, seeded tomato (about ½ large tomato)
> 1 tsp. minced garlic
> ⅛ tsp. plus a pinch of kosher salt
> 1 large egg
> 1 tsp. grated mozzarella cheese

1. Spray the inside of a 16-oz. mug with cooking spray.

2. Add the spinach, bread, tomato, garlic, and ⅛ tsp. of salt to a small bowl and use your hands to mix together. Pour into the mug and press down firmly.

3. Crack the egg into a small bowl and pour on top of the bread mixture. Sprinkle with the remaining pinch of salt and the cheese (there should be an inch or two of room at the top of the mug).

4. Cover and microwave until the egg has cooked through, about 2 minutes.

BREAKFAST POLENTA WITH BERRIES

Feel free to vary the type of frozen fruit in this breakfast treat—though don't use fresh. The liquid in the frozen berries helps to keep the dish moist. Be sure to use high-quality preserves. If you like, add a dollop of sour cream as a topping.

> ½ cup frozen mixed berries (not defrosted)
> 1 Tbs. berry preserves (any flavor)
> About ½ tube precooked polenta, cut into ½-inch-thick rounds
> ¼ plus ⅛ tsp. ground cinnamon
> 1 Tbs. milk
> 1 tsp. maple syrup or honey

1. Mix together the berries and preserves in a small bowl.

2. Place one polenta round in a 16-oz. mug and sprinkle with ⅛ tsp. of the cinnamon. Spoon one-third of the berry mixture on top. Repeat the layering two more times, using up all of the polenta, cinnamon, and berries. Press down the layers and cover. Microwave until hot, about 4 minutes.

3. Drizzle with the milk and syrup.

• • • • • • • • • • • • • • •

RASPBERRY OATMEAL WITH MAPLE SYRUP

Because the fresh berries are cooked, this is a great recipe for using up bruised or less fresh fruit. Be sure to opt for quick-cooking oats for this delicious, summertime breakfast.

> 1 cup milk
> ½ cup quick-cooking oats
> ½ cup packed fresh raspberries
> 2 Tbs. maple syrup
> ¼ tsp. ground cinnamon
> ⅛ tsp. kosher salt

1. In a small bowl, stir together all of the ingredients, and pour into a 16-oz. mug.

2. Cover and microwave until the oats are cooked, about 2 minutes.

SAUSAGE AND BISCUIT CRUMBLE

Try serving this strata-like breakfast with applesauce, maple syrup, or sautéed apples. You can substitute cooked crumbled bacon for the sausage if you like. If you're in a rush, skip the chives.

Nonstick cooking spray
1 cup chopped biscuit (about 1)
½ cup chopped browned chicken apple breakfast sausage
   (about 4 small links)
2 Tbs. shredded Cheddar cheese
1 Tbs. milk
1 Tbs. minced fresh chives
1 large egg
4 grinds black pepper

1. Grease the inside of a 16-oz. mug with cooking spray.

2. Add the biscuit and sausage pieces, cheese, milk, chives, egg, and pepper to a small bowl. Mix well with a fork.

3. Pour the egg mixture into the mug, cover, and microwave until the egg is cooked through, about 2 minutes.

KITCHEN SINK EGGS WITH VEGETABLES

Here's a delicious, easy way to incorporate vegetables into your diet:
a colorful egg breakfast. Make sure to stir the eggs halfway through,
as the eggs at the center and bottom take more time to cook.

Nonstick cooking spray
½ cup shredded cheese, such as mozzarella or Monterey Jack
2 large eggs
**1 cup assorted mixed vegetables, such as diced seeded tomato,
finely chopped fresh spinach leaves, ½-inch slices trimmed
fresh asparagus, and thawed frozen peas**
¼ tsp. kosher salt
5 grinds black pepper

1. Grease the inside of a 12-oz. mug with cooking spray.

2. Combine all of the ingredients in a bowl, mix well, and pour
into the mug.

3. Cover and microwave until the eggs are fully cooked, stirring
halfway through, about 3½ minutes.

SCRAMBLED EGGS WITH HAM AND SWISS

Vary these scrambled eggs with a myriad of ingredients. Omit the ham (just add a bit more salt) or substitute it with bacon bits or diced cooked breakfast sausage. Try different cheeses, such as Cheddar or goat. For a Mexican variation, stir in cooked chopped chorizo sausage, Cheddar, chili powder, and sliced scallions.

Nonstick cooking spray
½ cup ¼-inch-dice thinly sliced deli ham
3 Tbs. shredded Swiss cheese
2 large eggs
1 tsp. Dijon mustard
⅛ tsp. kosher salt
3 grinds black pepper
Minced fresh chives or flat-leaf parsley leaves (optional)

1. Spray the inside of a 16-oz. mug with cooking spray.

2. In a small bowl, stir together all of the ingredients and pour into the mug.

3. Cover and microwave for 1½ minutes. Use a fork to break up the egg mixture, then re-cover and microwave until the eggs are fully cooked, about 30 seconds more (check after 15 seconds). If desired, garnish with fresh herbs.

WARM CEREAL-TOPPED FRUIT COMPOTE

This nourishing breakfast tastes like a dessert! Vary this idea with other types of fruit. For a veritable treat, sweeten the cereal topping.

½ cup fresh white peach slices (about 1 peach)
½ cup fresh blueberries
1 tsp. maple syrup
⅛ tsp. kosher salt
⅛ tsp. ground cinnamon
½ cup unsweetened cereal flakes, such as Corn Flakes®
2 Tbs. slivered almonds

1. Stir together the peaches, blueberries, syrup, salt, and cinnamon in a small to medium bowl, then pour into a 16-oz. mug.

2. Cover and microwave until warm and tender, about 2 minutes.

3. Sprinkle the cereal and nuts on top. Re-cover and microwave until the topping is slightly warm, about another 45 seconds.

• • • • • • • • • • • • • • •

PINEAPPLE COCONUT OATMEAL

Feel free to swap in frozen mango chunks for the pineapple. Either way, this is a tropical-flavored breakfast!

1 cup canned light coconut milk, well shaken
½ cup frozen pineapple chunks
½ cup quick-cooking oats
1 Tbs. shredded unsweetened coconut
2 tsp. maple syrup
⅛ tsp. kosher salt
1 Tbs. finely chopped cashews

1. Stir together the coconut milk, pineapple, oats, coconut, syrup, and salt in a small to medium bowl. Pour into a 16-oz. mug.

2. Cover and microwave until creamy, about 3½ minutes. Sprinkle with the nuts.

WHOLE-GRAIN OAT BERRY MUFFIN

This wholesome breakfast muffin is low-sugar, completely whole-grain, and chock full of antioxidant-rich blueberries. Since the berries become incredibly hot and almost molten, wait a few minutes before serving. If you like, top with a dollop of Greek yogurt and a drizzle of honey. White whole-wheat flour is a pale, milder version of traditional whole-wheat flour, but if you can't find it, use traditional whole-wheat flour.

Nonstick cooking spray
¼ cup plus ½ tsp. white whole-wheat flour
3 Tbs. quick-cooking oats
½ tsp. baking powder
¼ tsp. ground cinnamon
⅛ tsp. kosher salt
¼ cup milk
2 Tbs. safflower oil
1 large egg
1 Tbs. honey
½ tsp. pure vanilla extract
3 Tbs. fresh blueberries

1. Spray the inside of a 16-oz. mug with cooking spray.

2. In a small bowl, use a fork to whisk together ¼ cup of the flour, the oats, baking powder, cinnamon, and salt.

3. Whisk together the milk, oil, egg, honey, and vanilla in a small bowl. Pour the dry ingredients into the wet and mix just until combined.

4. In a small bowl, toss the berries with the remaining ½ tsp. flour and add to the batter. Mix just until combined. Pour into the mug.

5. Cover and microwave until just cooked through in the center, about 2½ minutes (do not overcook).

POACHED EGG WITH WHOLE-WHEAT TOAST

For a two-egg portion, poach another egg separately following the same directions. This dish is a little heartier—and more colorful—with the chives, avocado, and chopped tomato.

> 1 large egg
> 1 slice whole-wheat bread, toasted
> 1 pinch of kosher salt
> 2 grinds black pepper
> Minced fresh chives, sliced avocado, or small-dice tomato (optional)

1. Add ½ cup water to a 12-oz. mug. Gently crack the egg into the water (it should be submerged). Cover with a relatively heavy microwave-safe ramekin or jar that will fit inside the mug and stay put on top of the egg, pressing it down (I use a glass jam jar).

2. Microwave until the white is completely opaque and cooked through but the yolk is still molten, about 1 minute 45 seconds (check after 1 minute). (Cook a bit longer if you have a compromised immune system or are cooking for someone who is pregnant, elderly, or very young.)

3. Place a clean towel on the counter. With a spoon, carefully transfer the poached egg to the towel to drain. Place the toast on a plate and top with the poached egg. Sprinkle the egg with the salt and pepper and top with the chives, avocado, and tomato, if desired.

BREAKFAST BROWN RICE WITH DATES AND PISTACHIOS

This Mideastern-inspired rice is not only ideal for breakfast, but also makes a healthful snack or dessert. Feel free to swap in cooked white rice for the brown rice, nondairy milk for the cow's milk, and golden raisins for the dates.

¾ cup cooked brown rice (long or short grain)
¼ cup milk
3 Tbs. fresh orange juice
1 Tbs. plus 1 tsp. finely chopped dates (about 2 large)
¾ tsp. fresh orange zest
½ tsp. maple syrup
⅛ tsp. ground cinnamon
⅛ tsp. ground cardamom
⅛ tsp. kosher salt
1½ Tbs. pistachios, lightly toasted and finely chopped

1. Stir together all of the ingredients except for the pistachios in a small to medium bowl and pour into a 16-oz. mug.

2. Cover and microwave until the dish is hot, about 2 minutes. Top with the pistachios.

MORNING GLORY MUFFIN

Full of carrots, pineapple, raisins, coconut, and pecans, this moist muffin will please adults and kids alike. Feel free to play around with this recipe and substitute dried cranberries for the raisins and walnuts for the pecans. For a more elegant presentation, you can invert this muffin onto a plate.

Nonstick cooking spray
¼ cup plus 1 Tbs. all-purpose flour
½ tsp. baking powder
¼ tsp. ground cinnamon
⅛ tsp. kosher salt
3 Tbs. maple syrup
2 Tbs. packed finely grated carrots (about ⅔ medium carrot)
2 Tbs. packed canned crushed pineapple in juice, drained
2 Tbs. vegetable oil
1 large egg
1 Tbs. finely chopped raisins
1 Tbs. shredded sweetened coconut
1 Tbs. finely chopped toasted pecans (about 5)

1. Spray the inside of a 16-oz. mug with cooking spray.

2. Combine the flour, baking powder, cinnamon, and salt in a small bowl and stir well with a fork. In a small to medium bowl, whisk together the syrup, carrots, pineapple, oil, egg, raisins, and coconut. Add the dry mixture to the wet mixture and stir just until well mixed (do not overmix). Pour into the mug.

3. Cover and microwave until cooked through in the center, about 2½ minutes. Sprinkle with the nuts (or invert onto a plate first and sprinkle the nuts over the top).

BREAKFAST BAR WITH QUINOA, OATS, NUTS, AND FRUIT

Try varying this recipe with other types of cooked grains, nuts, and dried fruit. Double the ingredients and split between two mugs to make more than one bar.

    Nonstick cooking spray
    2 Tbs. quick-cooking oats
    2 Tbs. cooked quinoa
    2 Tbs. finely chopped pistachios
    2 Tbs. sweetened dried cherries
    2 Tbs. vegetable oil
    2 Tbs. honey
    ¼ tsp. kosher salt

1. Spray the inside of a 12-oz. mug with cooking spray. Stir together all of the ingredients in a small to medium bowl, then pour into the mug.

2. Cover and microwave until the oats are cooked, about 3 minutes.

3. Pour the hot mixture onto a piece of parchment or waxed paper, shaping into a rectangle or narrow traditional bar. Chill until cold and solid, 30 minutes or more.

SAVORY SUMMER CORN OATMEAL WITH BACON

This oatmeal is surprisingly smoky, salty, and fresh at the same time. If you don't eat pork, just add a bit more salt or opt for finely chopped cooked turkey bacon.

- 1 cup milk
- ½ cup quick-cooking oats
- 1 Tbs. bacon bits (from 1 strip of bacon or packaged bits)
- 1 Tbs. shredded Cheddar cheese
- 1 Tbs. minced fresh chives
- ⅛ tsp. kosher salt
- 3 grinds black pepper
- Hot sauce

1. Stir together all of the ingredients except the hot sauce in a small bowl, then pour into a 16-oz. mug.

2. Cover and microwave until the oats are cooked, about 2½ minutes. Drizzle with hot sauce to taste.

● ● ● ● ● ● ● ● ● ● ● ● ● ●

BREAKFAST SAUSAGE WITH GRITS

Try drizzling with hot sauce and sprinkling with chives or chopped scallions.

- ¼ cup instant or quick-cooking (5-minute) grits
- 2 chicken apple breakfast sausages (about 1½ oz. total), each cut into four ½-inch pieces (heaping ¼ cup)
- 1 Tbs. unsalted butter
- ⅛ tsp. kosher salt
- 2 grinds black pepper

1. Combine all of the ingredients plus ¾ cup water in a 16-oz. mug.

2. Cook, uncovered, until the grits are creamy and tender, about 4 minutes.

SAUSAGE AND CHEESE BREAKFAST SANDWICH

This sandwich tastes like a decadent breakfast pastry. For the classic fast-food version, prepare using a buttermilk biscuit. After inverting onto a plate, drizzle with a bit of maple syrup and sprinkle with minced chives or sliced scallions if you like.

1 burger bun or buttermilk biscuit, split
2 chicken apple breakfast sausages (about 1½ oz. total), each cut into four ½-inch pieces (heaping ¼ cup)
2 Tbs. shredded Cheddar cheese
1 tsp. maple syrup
2 tsp. milk
Minced fresh chives or thinly sliced scallions (optional)

1. Place one bun half on the bottom of a 12-oz. mug. Top with half of the sausage pieces, half of the cheese, half of the maple syrup, and half of the milk. Repeat the layers one more time.

2. Cover and microwave until the cheese is melted, about 3 minutes. Garnish with the chives or scallions, if you like.

LUNCH & DINNER

NACHOS WITH REFRIED BEANS AND AVOCADO

Think of these microwave nachos as a tortilla casserole. Feel free to customize with the salsa and toppings of your choice and to swap in guacamole for the fresh avocado. To cut down on sodium, use low- or no-salt refried beans and salsa.

Nonstick cooking spray
½ cup canned refried beans
3 Tbs. high-quality salsa
10 tortilla chips, plus more for serving, if desired
3 Tbs. shredded Mexican cheese blend
½ avocado, diced (about ¼ cup)
1 tsp. sour cream, for garnish (optional)
1 tsp. canned green chiles, for garnish (optional)
1 tsp. thinly sliced trimmed scallions, for garnish (optional)

1. Spray the inside of a 12-oz. mug with cooking spray.

2. In a small bowl, stir together the beans and salsa.

3. Place half of the chips in the mug and top with a third of the cheese and half of the bean-salsa mixture. Top with the remaining chips, another third of the cheese, and the remaining bean mixture. Top with the remaining cheese.

4. Cover and microwave until most of the cheese melts, about 1 minute. Uncover and microwave until the remainder of the cheese melts, about another 30 seconds. Top with the avocado and other garnishes, and serve with additional chips, if desired.

WHITE BEAN "GRATIN" WITH OLIVES AND LEMON

Think of this light vegetarian entrée as a cross between a gratin and a bean dip. Try swapping in sun-dried tomatoes or roasted red peppers for the olives. If you don't have white beans, opt for pinto or garbanzo. Zest the lemon before juicing it.

1 cup (about 13 oz.) salt-free canned white beans (such as Great Northern or cannellini), rinsed and drained
1 tsp. fresh lemon zest
1 tsp. fresh lemon juice
2½ tsp. olive oil
¼ tsp. kosher salt
¼ tsp. dried oregano
1 Tbs. finely chopped pitted black or green olives (about 8)
2 Tbs. plain whole-wheat breadcrumbs
Cut-up vegetables (such as carrots and fennel) and breadsticks for dipping

1. In a small bowl, stir together the beans, zest, juice, 2 tsp. of the oil, kosher salt, and oregano. Mash until a rough paste forms. Add to a 12-oz. mug and top with the olives, breadcrumbs, and remaining oil.

2. Cover and microwave until hot, about 1 minute. Serve with vegetables and breadsticks.

PULLED BARBECUE CHICKEN
WITH CORNBREAD CRUMBS

Here's an almost-instant way to satisfy a barbecue craving while
using up leftover rotisserie chicken. For a heartier portion, go with
1 full cup of chicken. Make sure to use a high-quality barbecue sauce
since it's such a key part of this recipe.

> ½ cup packed shredded rotisserie or roast chicken
> (skin removed)
> 3 Tbs. barbecue sauce
> 1 Tbs. finely chopped fresh cilantro leaves
> 1 Tbs. thinly sliced trimmed scallions
> 1 Tbs. frozen corn, thawed
> 1 slice (roughly 1 inch thick) cornbread

1. In a small bowl, stir together the chicken, barbecue sauce,
cilantro, scallions, and corn. Pour into a 12-oz. mug and crumble
the cornbread on top.

2. Cover and microwave until hot, about 1 minute.

. . . .

HOT DOG WITH HONEY MUSTARD
AND CHEESE

Try topping with some pickle relish, sauerkraut, and diced red onions
for more color and tang. Or serve over half a hot dog bun.

> 1 hot dog, cut into 8 slices
> ¼ cup shredded Swiss or mozzarella cheese
> 2 Tbs. honey mustard

1. Mix together all of the ingredients in a 12-oz. mug.

2. Cover and cook until the hot dog is hot and the cheese is melted,
about 2½ minutes.

CHINESE BROWN RICE SALAD WITH EDAMAME

To add even more protein to this nourishing dish—which is also delicious chilled—stir in some diced extra-firm tofu. For a prettier presentation, pour the salad onto a plate.

1 Tbs. thinly sliced trimmed scallions (dark green parts only)
2 tsp. unseasoned rice vinegar
2 tsp. low-sodium soy sauce
1 tsp. honey
⅛ tsp. minced garlic
⅛ tsp. grated fresh ginger
½ cup packed cooked brown rice, short or long grain
⅓ cup packed frozen edamame, thawed
2 Tbs. finely grated peeled carrots
2 Tbs. small-dice red bell peppers

1. In a small bowl, stir together the scallions, rice vinegar, soy sauce, honey, garlic, and ginger, then stir in the remaining ingredients. Pour into a 12-oz. mug.

2. Cover and microwave until warm, about 1 minute.

CHICKEN MOLE BURRITO

Mole is a traditional sauce from Oaxaca, Mexico. Although the cocoa powder might sound odd, it imparts a rich, deep flavor. To keep the dish even simpler, substitute 3 Tbs. of salsa for the tomato paste, juice, chiles, and red onions. Try garnishing with pico de gallo, sour cream, or guacamole—or a combination. Feel free to use any leftover roast or rotisserie chicken.

1 Tbs. tomato paste
1 Tbs. canned green chiles
1 Tbs. finely chopped red onions
2 tsp. raisins
2 tsp. slivered almonds
1 tsp. honey
1 tsp. fresh lime juice
¼ tsp. unsweetened cocoa powder
⅛ tsp. kosher salt
½ cup shredded rotisserie or roast chicken (skin removed)
One 6-inch wheat tortilla

1. Add the tomato paste, chiles, onions, raisins, almonds, honey, lime juice, cocoa powder, and salt to a small bowl and stir well. Stir in the chicken and pour into a 12-oz. mug.

2. Cover and microwave until warm, about 1 minute; let cool for 25 seconds.

3. Place the tortilla on a plate and cover with a damp paper towel or clean kitchen towel. Microwave until warm, about 20 seconds.

4. Pour the chicken mixture onto the tortilla and roll up into a burrito.

WARM PEANUT NOODLES WITH SCALLIONS

These noodles are a true crowd-pleaser and will even win over kids! They're delicious warm or cold. Be sure to boil the pasta in plenty of salted water.

Nonstick cooking spray
2 Tbs. creamy peanut butter
1 Tbs. unseasoned rice vinegar
1 tsp. sesame oil
1 tsp. low-sodium soy sauce
1 tsp. honey
2 tsp. thinly sliced trimmed scallions (dark green parts only)
⅛ tsp. grated fresh ginger
1½ cups packed cooked whole-wheat fettuccini or linguini
1 Tbs. toasted peanuts, finely chopped

1. Spray the inside of a 12-oz. mug with cooking spray.

2. Add the peanut butter, vinegar, oil, soy sauce, honey, half of the scallions, and ginger to the mug and stir well.

3. Cover and microwave until smooth, about 30 seconds; stir. Stir in the noodles, cover, and microwave until warm, about another minute. Top with the remaining scallions and peanuts.

SHRIMP WITH GARLIC, LEMON & PARSLEY

Serve this restaurant-quality dinner-for-one over couscous, rice, or polenta. Pour the shrimp and sauce onto a plate for an elegant presentation.

1 Tbs. lemon zest
1 tsp. fresh lemon juice
1 large garlic clove, minced (about 1 tsp.)
1 tsp. olive oil
⅛ tsp. kosher salt
1/16 tsp. crushed red pepper flakes
6 oz. peeled and deveined large shrimp, tails left on
   (about eight 21- to 25-count shrimp)
1 Tbs. finely chopped fresh flat-leaf parsley leaves

1. In a small bowl, stir together the zest and juice, the garlic, oil, salt, and red pepper flakes. Add the shrimp and mix well. Pour into a 16-oz. mug.

2. Cover and microwave until the shrimp become pink and opaque, about 2 minutes. If they're not completely cooked, re-cover and microwave for another 15 to 30 seconds. Stir in the parsley.

PIZZA TOSS

This easy crowd-pleaser—think pizza in a mug, in less than
5 minutes—will become one of your go-to dishes. My kids request
it all the time. Be sure to use a high-quality marinara sauce.

> 1 cup 1-inch cubes country bread, such as ciabatta
> ½ cup high-quality marinara sauce
> ½ cup shredded mozzarella cheese
> ½ cup coarsely chopped fresh spinach leaves, washed
> and patted dry

1. Stir together all of the ingredients in a small bowl, then pour
into a 12-oz. mug. Pack down.

2. Cover and microwave until hot, about 2 minutes.

• • • • • • • • • • • • • •

MEATLOAF

This dish is so delicious, and if you serve it on a plate, no one will
know it was prepared in the microwave! Carefully place a plate over
the top of the mug and flip it over. Lift the mug and you will yield a
molded meatloaf. Slice it for sandwiches.

> 1 cup (about 6 oz.) cooked ground beef
> ¼ cup whole-wheat breadcrumbs
> 3 Tbs. ketchup
> 1 Tbs. finely chopped fresh flat-leaf parsley leaves
> 1 Tbs. finely grated carrots
> 2 tsp. finely chopped red onions
> 1 tsp. Dijon mustard
> 1 tsp. low-sodium soy sauce
> ½ tsp. dried thyme
> ⅛ tsp. kosher salt
> A few grinds of black pepper

1. In a small bowl, stir together all of the ingredients, and pour into
a 16-oz. mug. Pack down.

2. Cover and microwave until hot, about 2 minutes.

CORNBREAD STUFFING WITH BLACK BEANS

Feel free to top this colorful entrée with a dollop of sour cream. If you're out of cornbread, try country bread, but cut off the crust. Match the salsa to your preferred level of heat—very spicy or mild.

Nonstick cooking spray
1 cup 1-inch cubes cornbread
½ cup canned black beans, rinsed and drained
½ cup salsa
¼ cup shredded Cheddar or Mexican cheese blend
2 heaping Tbs. thinly sliced trimmed scallions

1. Spray the inside of a 16-oz. mug with cooking spray.

2. In a small bowl, gently mix all of the ingredients and pour into the mug. Pack down.

3. Cover and microwave until hot, about 2 minutes.

• • • • • • • • • • • • •

PASTA PUTTANESCA

Consider heating up this pasta dish with a pinch of crushed red pepper flakes.

Nonstick cooking spray
1 cup cooked whole-wheat elbow macaroni
½ cup marinara sauce
¼ cup shredded mozzarella cheese
2 Tbs. finely chopped fresh flat-leaf parsley leaves
1 Tbs. rinsed jarred capers
1 Tbs. finely chopped pitted black or green olives (4 to 5)

1. Spray the inside of a 16-oz. mug with cooking spray.

2. In a small bowl, stir together all of the ingredients and pour into the mug.

3. Cover and microwave until the cheese melts, about 2 minutes.

BURRITO WITH REFRIED BEANS

Consider serving the bean-cheese mixture as a dip, with cut-up fresh veggies. To feed two people, prepare in a small to medium microwave-safe bowl, then spoon onto tortillas. For a lower-salt version, opt for no- or low-salt refried beans.

½ cup canned refried beans
¼ cup salsa, plus more for serving
2 Tbs. thinly sliced trimmed scallions
2 Tbs. shredded Mexican cheese blend
⅛ tsp. ground cumin
One 10-inch wheat tortilla
1 tsp. sour cream, for serving
1 tsp. guacamole, for serving

1. In a small bowl, stir together the beans, salsa, scallions, cheese, and cumin; pour into a 12-oz. mug.

2. Cover and microwave until the cheese melts, about 2 minutes.

3. Place the tortilla on a plate and cover with a damp paper towel or clean kitchen towel. Microwave until warm, about 20 seconds. Spoon the bean filling onto the tortilla and roll up. Serve with the sour cream, guacamole, and salsa.

SPRING FRIED RICE WITH ASPARAGUS

Try incorporating other vegetables and the Korean condiment gochujang into this quick Asian-inspired entrée. For those with compromised immune systems or who prefer their eggs fully cooked, microwave until the yolk is solid, 30 to 60 seconds longer.

1 cup cooked and cooled brown rice (short or long grain)
½ cup ½-inch-long slices fresh asparagus (about 4 spears, bottom few inches trimmed off)
1 Tbs. thinly sliced trimmed scallions (white and light green parts)
1 Tbs. plus 1 tsp. low-sodium soy sauce
1 Tbs. sesame oil
1 tsp. minced garlic
1 tsp. minced ginger
1 tsp. honey
1 tsp. unseasoned rice vinegar
1 large egg
Pinch of kosher salt

1. In a small bowl, stir together the rice, asparagus, scallions, soy sauce, oil, garlic, ginger, honey, and vinegar, and pour into a 12-oz. mug. Pack down.

2. Crack the egg over the top and sprinkle with salt. Cover and microwave until the egg is mostly cooked through, but if pricked still yields a molten yolk, 2½ to 3 minutes.

3. To eat, prick the yolk and let it bathe the rice and vegetables, serving as a sauce.

INDIAN RED BEANS OVER RICE

For a heftier portion, double the ingredients and use a 16-oz. mug. For a lower-sodium version, seek out low- or no-salt beans. Garam masala is an Indian spice mixture that can be found at most grocery stores.

½ cup canned small red beans, rinsed and drained
2 Tbs. finely chopped red onions
2 Tbs. finely chopped red bell peppers
2 tsp. finely chopped fresh cilantro or flat-leaf parsley leaves
1 tsp. fresh lime juice
1 tsp. tomato paste
½ tsp. honey
¼ tsp. garam masala
¼ tsp. kosher salt
½ cup cooked brown rice (short or long grain)

1. Mix together the beans, onions, bell peppers, herbs, lime juice, tomato paste, honey, garam masala, and salt in a small bowl. Pour into a 12-oz. mug.

2. Cover and microwave until hot, about 2 minutes. Serve over the rice.

POLENTA LASAGNA

Since this recipe is very elemental, use high-quality sauce. Feel free to garnish with finely chopped fresh oregano or basil leaves. You can find precooked polenta tubes near the pasta at most grocery stores. For a variation, try substituting large cooked ravioli squares for the polenta circles.

> **Nonstick cooking spray**
> **1 cup high-quality marinara sauce**
> **About ½ tube precooked polenta, cut into three ½-inch-thick rounds**
> **3 Tbs. plus 1 tsp. shredded mozzarella cheese**

1. Spray the inside of a 16-oz. mug with cooking spray.

2. Add ¼ cup of the sauce to the bottom of the mug, then add one round of the polenta, then 1 Tbs. of the cheese. Repeat layering two more times. Add the remaining ¼ cup of sauce, then the remaining 1 tsp. of cheese.

3. Cover and cook until hot, about 3 minutes.

• • • • • • • • • • • • •

SLOPPY JOE WITH PORK

Feel free to substitute a high-quality barbecue sauce for the ketchup and mustard, and cooked ground chicken, turkey, or beef for the pork. Crumbled seitan or rinsed and drained canned beans could also work.

> **1 cup cooked ground pork**
> **3 Tbs. ketchup**
> **2 Tbs. thinly sliced trimmed scallions**
> **1 Tbs. yellow mustard**
> **⅛ tsp. kosher salt**
> **1 whole-wheat burger bun, toasted**

1. In a small bowl, stir together the pork, ketchup, scallions, mustard, and salt; pour into a 16-oz. mug.

2. Cover and microwave until hot, about 2 minutes. Spoon onto the bottom half of the toasted bun, then cover with the top.

CLASSIC CHICKEN SOUP

Leftover chicken takes on a new life in this cozy soup. Since the ingredients are few, be sure to use a high-quality chicken broth. If you aren't using leftover noodles, cook the noodles in salted water for the shortest amount of time recommended on the package, usually about 3 minutes. Serve with toast or crackers.

1 cup chicken broth
½ cup shredded rotisserie or roast chicken (skin removed)
¼ cup very thinly sliced carrots (about ½ carrot)
¼ cup cooked small egg noodles
1 Tbs. plus 1 tsp. thinly sliced trimmed scallions (light green and dark green parts)
1 tsp. fresh lemon juice
⅛ tsp. kosher salt
2 grinds of black pepper
1 Tbs. finely chopped fresh dill

1. In a small bowl, stir together the broth, chicken, carrots, noodles, scallions, juice, salt, and pepper. Pour into a 16-oz. mug.

2. Cover and microwave until the carrots are tender, about 7 minutes. Stir in the dill.

CHICKEN AND PINEAPPLE BURRITO

Feel free to use any leftover rotisserie or roast chicken. Serve the burrito with plenty of toppings, such as guacamole, fresh cilantro, and sour cream. Be sure to use a high-quality salsa.

½ cup shredded rotisserie or roast chicken (skin removed)
3 Tbs. high-quality salsa
2 Tbs. canned black beans, rinsed and drained
2 Tbs. finely chopped red onions
2 Tbs. diced fresh pineapple
2 Tbs. finely chopped bell peppers, ideally half red
   and half green
¼ tsp. ground cumin
¼ tsp. kosher salt
One 6-inch wheat tortilla

1. In a small bowl, mix together all of the ingredients (except for the tortilla). Pour into a 12-oz. mug. Cover and microwave until hot and the onions are soft, about 2 minutes.

2. Place the tortilla on a plate and cover with a damp paper towel or clean kitchen towel. Microwave until warm, about 20 seconds. Spoon the filling onto the tortilla and roll up.

CHICKEN "POTPIE"

Use leftover roast chicken in this perfect-for-winter dish. For a vegetarian version, substitute rinsed and drained canned white beans for the chicken.

½ cup shredded rotisserie or roast chicken (skin removed)
½ cup frozen mixed vegetables (such as peas and carrots), thawed and drained
2 Tbs. shredded Cheddar cheese
3 Tbs. milk
1 Tbs. finely chopped fresh dill
¼ tsp. kosher salt
4 grinds of black pepper
½ biscuit, left intact or crumbled
⅛ tsp. paprika

1. In a small bowl, stir together the chicken, vegetables, cheese, 2 Tbs. of the milk, the dill, salt, and pepper. Pour into a 16-oz. mug and pack down. Top with the biscuit, then drizzle with the remaining 1 Tbs. of milk and sprinkle with the paprika.

2. Cover and microwave until the "potpie" is hot, about 3 minutes.

• • • • • • • • • • • • • •

PASTA, BEAN & TOMATO STEW WITH KALE

Try varying this healthful recipe with different types of beans and pasta. Choose a flavorful chicken broth and high-quality marinara sauce.

½ cup chicken broth
¼ cup cooked whole-wheat elbow macaroni
¼ cup very thinly sliced fresh kale leaves (stems removed)
¼ cup canned black beans, rinsed and drained
3 Tbs. marinara sauce
1 Tbs. finely grated Parmigiano-Reggiano or Parmesan cheese

1. In a small bowl, stir together the broth, pasta, kale, beans, and marinara sauce. Pour into a 16-oz. mug and top with the cheese.

2. Cover and microwave until the kale is tender, about 3 minutes.

CHICKEN AND SPAGHETTI

Chicken and spaghetti was one of my favorite childhood dishes, and I'm sure this version is a lot easier to make than the one my mom prepared. For starters, it's a delicious way to use up leftover roast chicken. If cooking the pasta, be sure the cooking water is well salted (though leftover pasta is fine too); also be sure to use a high-quality marinara sauce. For more color, garnish with finely chopped fresh parsley leaves. Consider stirring in some crushed red pepper flakes if you like a little heat.

Nonstick cooking spray
½ cup shredded rotisserie or roast chicken (skin removed)
½ cup cooked whole-wheat spaghetti
¼ cup marinara sauce
¼ cup shredded mozzarella cheese
¼ tsp. dried oregano
⅛ tsp. kosher salt

1. Spray the inside of a 12-oz. mug with cooking spray.

2. In a small bowl, stir together all of the ingredients, then pour into the mug.

3. Cover and microwave until hot, about 2 minutes.

MOROCCAN PUMPKIN AND CHICKPEA STEW

This vegetarian entrée is full of flavor. To make it vegan, swap agave nectar for the honey.

- ¾ cup low-sodium vegetable stock
- ½ cup canned pumpkin or butternut squash purée
- ½ cup canned chickpeas, rinsed and drained
- ¼ cup fresh spinach leaves, washed and patted dry
- 1 tsp. honey
- ⅛ tsp. ground cumin
- ⅛ tsp. ground coriander
- ⅛ tsp. ground cinnamon
- ⅛ tsp. kosher salt
- Toasted country bread, for serving

1. Combine the stock, pumpkin or squash, chickpeas, spinach, honey, cumin, coriander, cinnamon, and salt in a small bowl, then pour into a 16-oz. mug.

2. Cover and microwave until hot and the spinach is cooked through, 2 to 3 minutes. Serve with the bread.

PASTA WITH MELTED BUTTER AND CHEDDAR

Here's a lighter, quicker take on mac and cheese. Feel free to stir any of the following into the hot milk: ¼ tsp. mustard, ½ tsp. minced fresh chives, pinch of paprika, or a few grinds of black pepper. If you're not using leftover macaroni, be sure to cook it for slightly less than the recommended maximum cooking time; it should take about 6 minutes.

ΒΌ cup milk, ideally 2% or whole
½ cup shredded Cheddar cheese
1 Tbs. unsalted butter
⅛ tsp. kosher salt
1 cup cooked whole-wheat elbow macaroni

1. In a 12-oz. mug, microwave the milk until hot, about 30 seconds. Immediately stir in the cheese, butter, and salt until relatively smooth. Stir in the pasta.

2. Cover and microwave until the cheese melts and the pasta is warm, 2 to 3 minutes. Stir again.

TUNA NOODLE CASSEROLE

Feel free to gussy up the breadcrumb topping by mixing in finely chopped fresh parsley or dill.

> One 5-oz. can albacore tuna, packed in water (with no added salt), drained
> ½ cup cooked whole-wheat elbow macaroni
> 3 Tbs. shredded Cheddar or Swiss cheese
> 3 Tbs. milk
> 2 Tbs. thinly sliced trimmed scallions
> ½ tsp. Dijon mustard
> ⅛ tsp. kosher salt
> 3 grinds of black pepper
> 1 Tbs. plain whole-wheat breadcrumbs
> 1 tsp. olive oil

1. In a small bowl, stir together the tuna, pasta, cheese, milk, scallions, mustard, salt, and pepper, breaking up the tuna with a fork. Pour into a 12-oz. mug.

2. Cover and microwave until the cheese melts, about 2 minutes.

3. In a small bowl, stir together the breadcrumbs and oil. Sprinkle on top.

CHINESE CHICKEN WITH NOODLES AND BLACK BEAN SAUCE

Vary this recipe by using hoisin instead of black bean sauce (and omitting the honey). If you don't have leftover noodles and are cooking them for this recipe, be sure to cook in well-salted water for the minimum amount of time on the package, probably 3 minutes. Use any type of leftover roast chicken as long as it is neutral in flavor.

½ cup shredded rotisserie or roast chicken (skin removed)
½ cup frozen mixed vegetables (such as peas and carrots),
   thawed and drained
½ cup cooked small egg noodles
2 Tbs. chicken broth
1 Tbs. Chinese black bean sauce
½ tsp. honey
½ tsp. fresh lime juice

1. In a small bowl, stir together all of the ingredients, then pour into a 16-oz. mug and pack down.

2. Cover and microwave until hot, about 3 minutes.

PASTITSIO

A traditional Greek casserole of cooked pasta and ground meat, this version is lower in fat and easier to make. If you'd like, substitute a high-quality marinara sauce for the tomato paste and broth. Cook the pasta in salted water and use a high-quality chicken broth.

Nonstick cooking spray
¾ cup cooked whole-wheat elbow macaroni
½ cup cooked ground beef
¼ cup shredded mozzarella
3 Tbs. tomato paste
2 Tbs. chicken broth
⅛ tsp. dried thyme
⅛ tsp. ground cinnamon
Heaping ⅛ tsp. kosher salt
3 grinds of black pepper

1. Spray the inside of a 16-oz. mug with cooking spray.

2. In a small bowl, stir together all of the ingredients and pour into the mug.

3. Cover and microwave until the cheese melts, about 2 minutes.

• • • • • • • • • • • • • •

INDIAN TOFU AND PEAS

Here's a much simpler take on the traditional Indian dish mutter paneer (peas and paneer cheese). Use paneer cheese in place of the tofu if you can find it (look in the refrigerated section of grocery stores, near the tofu). Since this recipe is so elemental, opt for a high-quality curry sauce.

½ cup ¼-inch-dice extra-firm tofu, drained
½ cup frozen peas (not thawed)
¼ cup Indian curry simmer sauce
½ cup cooked rice

1. Stir together all of the ingredients in a small bowl and pour into a 16-oz. mug.

2. Cover and microwave until the peas are hot, about 3 minutes.

TOMATO SOUP WITH PARMESAN

If you prefer a richer soup, feel free to add about 2 Tbs. heavy cream. Other additions could be dried or finely chopped fresh oregano, thyme, or marjoram; small cooked noodles; or thawed frozen vegetables, such as peas. I love to use my Microplane to finely grate the cheese; however, you can also use the fine holes of a box grater. Make sure to use a high-quality marinara sauce.

> 1 cup marinara sauce
> ½ cup vegetable or chicken stock
> 1 tsp. fresh orange juice
> 1 tsp. unsalted butter (not melted)
> 1 Tbs. finely grated Parmigiano-Reggiano cheese
> 1 slice toasted or grilled country bread, such as ciabatta
>   (optional)

1. Place a 16-oz. mug on a plate. Add the marinara sauce, stock, juice, and butter to the mug and stir well.

2. Cover and microwave (on the plate) until the butter melts, about 3½ minutes. Sprinkle with the cheese and serve with the bread, if desired.

PORK WITH CORN AND SCALLIONS

Feel free to substitute cooked ground chicken, turkey, or beef if you
don't eat pork.

> 1 cup cooked ground pork
> ½ cup fresh or frozen, thawed, and drained corn kernels
> 2 Tbs. tomato paste
> 1 Tbs. plus 1 tsp. thinly sliced trimmed scallions
> 1 tsp. fresh lime juice
> ¼ tsp. kosher salt
> ⅛ tsp. ground cumin
> ⅛ tsp. chili powder
> 3 grinds of black pepper

1. In a small bowl, stir together all of the ingredients and pour into a
16-oz. mug.

2. Cover and microwave until the corn is tender, about 2½ minutes.

• • • • • • • • • • • • • •

SPICY ITALIAN LENTIL SOUP

Serve this comforting vegetarian soup with whole-grain toast
drizzled with olive oil. If your lentils are not low sodium, use only half
of the salt.

> ¾ cup vegetable broth
> ¾ cup canned low-sodium lentils, rinsed and drained
> ¼ cup finely grated carrots
> 1 Tbs. tomato paste
> ¼ tsp. dried oregano
> ¼ tsp. kosher salt
> ⅛ tsp. crushed red pepper flakes
> 3 grinds of black pepper

1. In a small bowl, stir together all of the ingredients and mash with
a potato masher. Pour into a 12-oz. mug.

2. Cover and microwave until the soup is hot, about 3 minutes.

MISO SOUP

You can find kombu and bonito in the Asian section of many grocery stores. Consider adding thawed frozen vegetables, such as peas or diced carrots, to this light lunch. Make sure to use a high-quality broth.

> 1 cup vegetable or chicken broth
> One 4-inch piece dried kombu seaweed, broken in half
> 1 Tbs. bonito (dried tuna) flakes
> ¼ cup ¼-inch-dice firm tofu
> 2 tsp. white or yellow miso
> 1 tsp. thinly sliced trimmed scallions (dark green parts only)

1. Combine the broth, kombu, and bonito in a 16-oz. mug.

2. Cover and microwave until very hot, about 2½ minutes. Pour into a fine-mesh strainer set over a small bowl, then carefully pour the strained broth back into the mug.

3. To the broth in the mug, stir in the tofu, miso, and scallions; whisk until the miso dissolves.

• • • • • • • • • • • • • •

"GRILLED" CHEESE

If you don't like mustard, feel free to omit it. Try other cheeses, such as shredded Swiss. For a more elaborate sandwich, you can even layer chopped corned beef with sauerkraut and shredded Swiss in the mug (try ¼ cup beef and 2 tsp. of sauerkraut). Minced fresh chives would be delicious on top of whatever variation you create.

> 1 hamburger bun, split
> 1 tsp. yellow deli mustard, divided
> ¼ cup shredded Cheddar cheese, divided
> 1 Tbs. milk

1. Divide the mustard between both bun halves, spreading it on evenly. Place one bun half in a 12-oz. mug, mustard side up. Top with half of the cheese. Place the other bun half on top, mustard side facing up. Top with the remaining cheese, and then pour the milk on top.

2. Cover and microwave until the cheese melts, about 3 minutes.

SPICY KOREAN MEATBALLS

Opt for meatballs in as neutral a flavor as possible. Gochujang sauce is available in the Asian section of most grocery stores. Serve these flavorful meatballs over cooked rice.

- 2 Tbs. Korean gochujang sauce
- ½ tsp. minced fresh ginger
- ½ tsp. fresh lime juice
- ½ tsp. low-sodium soy sauce
- ½ tsp. honey
- 4 frozen precooked meatballs (not thawed)

1. Whisk together the gochujang sauce, ginger, lime juice, soy sauce, and honey in a 12-oz. mug. Add the meatballs and stir to combine.

2. Cover and microwave until the centers of the meatballs are hot, 3 to 4 minutes.

• • • • • • • • • • • • • •

MEATBALL PARMESAN

A sprinkle of finely chopped fresh parsley or basil leaves over the meatballs would add color. Be sure to use a high-quality marinara sauce.

- ¼ cup plus 2 Tbs. marinara sauce
- 3 Tbs. shredded mozzarella cheese
- 1 Tbs. finely grated Parmigiano-Reggiano cheese
- 4 frozen precooked meatballs (not thawed)
- 1 hoagie roll, split open and toasted, or 1 slice toasted Italian bread, such as ciabatta, for serving

1. In a small to medium bowl, mix together the marinara sauce, both cheeses, and meatballs and pour into a 12-oz. mug.

2. Cover and microwave until the centers of the meatballs are hot, 3 to 4 minutes. Pour over the bread.

SPICY CHINESE TOFU AND VEGETABLES

Sriracha is available in the Asian section of most grocery stores. If you can't find it, use hot sauce instead. Feel free to try other frozen vegetables. If they're in very small pieces, reduce the initial cooking time to 2 to 3 minutes.

½ cup frozen stir-fry vegetables (not thawed)
¼ cup vegetable broth
½ cup ½-inch cubes extra-firm tofu, drained
1 Tbs. plus 1 tsp. low-sodium soy sauce
½ tsp. Sriracha sauce
½ tsp. fresh lime juice
½ tsp. honey
½ cup cooked rice, for serving

1. Place the vegetables and 2 Tbs. of the broth in a 12-oz. mug, cover, and microwave until the vegetables are hot, 3 to 4 minutes.

2. Gently stir in the remaining broth, the tofu, soy sauce, Sriracha, lime juice, and honey.

3. Re-cover and microwave until the tofu is hot, about another 1½ minutes. Serve over rice.

GREEK CAULIFLOWER WITH FETA

If you love olives, feel free to add them to this satisfying dish.

- Scant 1½ cups ½-inch raw cauliflower florets
- ½ cup marinara sauce
- 2 Tbs. crumbled feta cheese
- ¼ tsp. dried oregano
- Finely chopped fresh flat-leaf parsley leaves (optional)

1. In a small to medium bowl, stir together the cauliflower, marinara sauce, feta, and oregano and pour into a 16-oz. mug.

2. Cover and microwave until the cauliflower is tender, about 5 minutes. Top with the parsley, if desired.

· · · · · · · · · · · · · ·

WHITE BEAN, ARTICHOKE & SUN-DRIED TOMATO TOSS

Toss this flavorful vegetarian dish with cooked pasta (such as gnocchi) or serve over toasted country bread.

- ½ cup canned white beans, rinsed and drained
- ½ cup canned artichoke hearts (about 4), drained and halved
- ¼ cup coarsely chopped sun-dried tomatoes packed in oil, drained
- 1 Tbs. pesto
- 1½ tsp. lemon zest
- ⅛ tsp. kosher salt
- 3 grinds of black pepper

1. In a small to medium bowl, stir together the ingredients and pour into a 16-oz. mug.

2. Cover and microwave until hot, about 2 minutes.

THAI CURRIED PUMPKIN BISQUE

Slightly spicy and sweet, this rich and creamy bisque is impressive and delicious. This recipe makes one generous portion. For a smaller amount, cut all of the ingredients in half and prepare in a 16-oz. mug (still microwave for 5 minutes).

> 1 cup ½-inch raw cauliflower florets
> ½ cup low-sodium vegetable broth
> ½ cup canned pumpkin or butternut squash purée
> ¼ cup canned coconut milk (full fat), well shaken
> ¼ cup finely chopped red or green bell peppers
> 1 Tbs. plus 1 tsp. Thai green curry paste
> 1 Tbs. thinly sliced trimmed scallions
> ½ tsp. honey
> ⅛ tsp. kosher salt

1. In a medium bowl, stir together all of the ingredients and pour into a 20-oz. mug. (Alternatively, microwave in a microwave-safe bowl.)

2. Cover and microwave until the vegetables are tender, about 5 minutes.

• • • • • • • • • • • • •

BROCCOLI AND WHITE BEAN MARINARA

Try this vegetarian dish served over a slice of toasted country bread, such as ciabatta. If you like, grate some Parmesan cheese over the top. For heat, add a pinch of crushed red pepper flakes.

> 1 cup ½-inch raw broccoli florets
> ½ cup marinara sauce
> ½ cup canned white beans, rinsed and drained
> 1½ tsp. lemon zest

1. In a small to medium bowl, stir together all of the ingredients and pour into a 16-ounce mug.

2. Cover and microwave until the broccoli is tender, 4 to 5 minutes.

CLASSIC SHEPHERD'S PIE

If you don't have leftover mashed potatoes, make some for this dish and save the rest for another use. Prick a medium-sized Idaho or Russet potato all over with a fork and microwave until tender, about 10 minutes. Carefully slice in half and transfer the flesh to a small bowl (snack on the skin). Mash with a potato masher until smooth, and stir in 1 Tbs. of olive oil, ¼ tsp. kosher salt, and a few grinds of black pepper.

> 1 cup (about 6 oz.) cooked ground beef
> 2 Tbs. finely chopped red onions
> 1 Tbs. finely grated carrots
> 1 tsp. Dijon mustard
> ½ tsp. dried rosemary
> ⅛ tsp. kosher salt
> 1 cup mashed potatoes
> 1 tsp. shredded Cheddar cheese

1. In a small bowl, mix together the ground beef, onions, carrots, mustard, rosemary, and salt. Pour into a 16-oz. mug. Place the mashed potatoes on top, pressing them down. Sprinkle with the cheese.

2. Cover and microwave until warm and the cheese melts, about 2 minutes.

BEEF AND BEAN CHILI

Choose a high-quality salsa for this recipe. If you're vegetarian, omit the meat and double the beans. For a low-sodium variation, use low- or no-salt beans.

½ cup canned black or pinto beans, rinsed and drained
½ cup (about 3 oz.) cooked ground beef
½ cup high-quality salsa
1 tsp. thinly sliced trimmed scallions
¼ tsp. kosher salt
1 tsp. finely chopped fresh cilantro leaves
About 6 tortilla chips
1 tsp. guacamole, for serving
1 tsp. sour cream, for serving

1. In a small bowl, stir together the beans, ground beef, salsa, scallions, and salt, and pour into a 12-oz. mug.

2. Cover and microwave until hot, about 2 minutes.

3. Sprinkle with the cilantro and insert chips around the edges. Serve with the guacamole and sour cream.

MEXICAN VEGGIE BURGER

More salsa would be a fitting accompaniment. Instead of serving with avocado slices, mash the avocado with a bit of lime juice and kosher salt and spread it on top of the burger.

½ cup canned pinto beans, rinsed and drained
¼ cup plain whole-wheat breadcrumbs
¼ cup salsa
¼ cup finely grated carrots
1 Tbs. thinly sliced trimmed scallions
½ avocado, sliced
Hamburger bun, for serving (optional)

1. In a medium bowl, mash together the pinto beans, breadcrumbs, salsa, carrots, and scallions with a potato masher. With your hands, shape into a ball and place in a 16-oz. mug.

2. Cover and microwave until the scallions are soft and the burger is hot, about 2 minutes. Top with the avocado slices. If you like, serve on a hamburger bun.

CLASSIC AMERICAN VEGGIE BURGER

Instead of serving this burger with the typical accompaniments, here you'll add them to the mix. The result: You'll get the classic burger flavors without having to prep—and clean up—a lot of ingredients.

    ½ cup canned pinto beans, rinsed and drained
    ¼ cup plain whole-wheat breadcrumbs
    2 Tbs. ketchup
    1 Tbs. minced red onions
    1 tsp. deli-style yellow mustard
    ⅛ tsp. kosher salt
    3 grinds of black pepper

1. In a small to medium bowl, mash together all of the ingredients with a potato masher. With your hands, shape into a ball and place in a 16-oz. mug.

2. Cover and microwave until the onions are soft, about 3 minutes.

• • • • • • • • • • • • • •

BLACK BEANS WITH FETA AND TOMATOES

Dip tortilla chips into this Greek-Mexican dip-like entrée.

    ½ cup canned salt-free black beans, rinsed and drained
    ¼ cup cored, seeded, and chopped tomato (about ½)
    3 Tbs. salsa
    2 Tbs. crumbled feta
    2 tsp. thinly sliced trimmed scallions
    ⅛ tsp. kosher salt

1. Stir together all of the ingredients in a small bowl, then pour into a 12-oz. mug.

2. Cover and microwave until the scallions are tender and the dish is hot, about 3 minutes.

PUMPKIN-ORANGE SOUP WITH WHITE BEANS AND SAGE

Try crumbling some amaretti (almond) cookies on top—a flavorful change from croutons. For a vegan take, opt for the vegetable broth and maple syrup.

> ½ cup canned pumpkin or butternut squash purée
> ½ cup low-sodium vegetable or chicken broth
> ¼ cup canned white beans, rinsed and drained
> 1 Tbs. orange juice
> ¾ tsp. maple syrup or honey
> ¼ tsp. minced fresh sage leaves
> ½ tsp. orange zest
> ⅛ tsp. kosher salt
> 3 grinds of black pepper

1. Stir together all of the ingredients in a small to medium bowl, then pour into a 16-oz. mug.

2. Cover and microwave until hot, about 3 minutes.

• • • • • • • • • • • • •

QUINOA SALAD WITH TOMATO AND PESTO

Using half red and half white quinoa makes for a prettier salad. Feel free to leave out the mozzarella and to swap in rinsed and drained canned white beans.

> ¾ cup cooked quinoa
> ¼ cup cored, seeded, and diced ripe tomato (about ½)
> ¼ cup ⅓-inch raw cauliflower florets
> 2 Tbs. pesto
> 2 Tbs. grated mozzarella cheese

1. In a small to medium bowl, stir together all of the ingredients, then pour into a 16-oz. mug.

2. Cover and microwave until the cauliflower is tender, about 4 minutes.

INDIAN BROWN RICE WITH MANGO CHUTNEY AND CHICKPEAS

Mango chutney instantly adds Indian flair to this dish. If you like cilantro, stir some—finely chopped—into this slightly sweet, high-protein meal.

    ¾ cup cooked brown rice (short or long grain)
    ½ cup canned chickpeas, rinsed and drained
    ¼ cup finely chopped orange bell peppers
    2 Tbs. mango chutney
    1 Tbs. thinly sliced trimmed scallions
    ⅛ tsp. kosher salt

1. Stir together all of the ingredients in a small to medium bowl, then pour into a 16-oz. mug.

2. Cover and microwave until the peppers are tender, about 4 minutes.

• • • • • • • • • • • • • •

COCONUT RICE WITH CHICKPEAS AND GARAM MASALA

This aromatic rice is nice topped with plain yogurt.

    ¾ cup cooked brown rice (short or long grain)
    ½ cup canned chickpeas, rinsed and drained
    ¼ cup canned coconut milk (full or low fat), well shaken
    2 Tbs. unsweetened coconut flakes
    1 Tbs. mango chutney
    1 Tbs. thinly sliced trimmed scallions
    1 tsp. golden raisins
    ¼ tsp. garam masala
    ⅛ tsp. kosher salt

1. In a small to medium bowl, stir together all of the ingredients; pour into a 16-oz. mug.

2. Cover and microwave until the scallions are tender, about 4 minutes.

MEXICAN QUINOA WITH CORN AND BROCCOLI

Finely chopped fresh cilantro would be a delicious and colorful addition. If you eat vegan or are sensitive to dairy, feel free to swap rinsed and drained canned pinto beans for the cheese.

- ¾ cup cooked quinoa
- ¼ cup cored, seeded, and diced ripe tomato (about ½ tomato)
- ¼ cup ⅓-inch raw broccoli florets
- ¼ cup raw corn kernels (from 1 small ear)
- 2 Tbs. salsa
- 2 Tbs. grated Mexican cheese blend
- ⅛ tsp. kosher salt
- 1 Tbs. finely chopped fresh cilantro leaves

1. In a small to medium bowl, stir together all of the ingredients, then pour into a 16-oz. mug.

2. Cover and microwave until the broccoli is tender, about 4 minutes.

• • • • • • • • • • • • • •

CORN SOUP WITH BACON AND CHIVES

You'll swear this soup was simmering for hours. Substitute thinly sliced scallions if you can't find chives. If your grocer doesn't stock prepared corn soup, try pumpkin or tomato.

- 1 cup canned corn soup
- 2 Tbs. minced chives
- 1 Tbs. plus 1 tsp. crumbled cooked bacon (about 2 strips)
    or 2 tsp. bacon bits
- 3 grinds of black pepper
- Scant ¼ tsp. kosher salt

1. Stir together all of the ingredients in a 12-oz. mug.

2. Cover and microwave until hot, about 3 minutes.

ZUCCHINI AND RICOTTA LASAGNA

This dish is messy and best eaten in the mug, but it is delicious!
Substitute finely grated carrots for some of the zucchini if you like.

3 Tbs. part-skim ricotta cheese
2 tsp. grated Parmesan cheese
1 sheet no-boil lasagna (roughly 5½ x 2½ inches), broken
    into about six 1-inch pieces
¾ cup marinara sauce
½ cup grated unpeeled zucchini (about ⅔ medium zucchini)

1. In a small bowl, stir together the ricotta and Parmesan.

2. In a 16-oz. mug, layer the ingredients in this order: 2 pieces of
lasagna, 2 Tbs. sauce, 1 Tbs. cheese, 2 Tbs. sauce, ¼ cup zucchini,
2 Tbs. sauce, 2 pieces of lasagna, 1 Tbs. cheese, 2 Tbs. sauce, the
remaining ¼ cup zucchini, 2 Tbs. sauce, the remaining 2 lasagna
pieces, the remaining 1 Tbs. cheese, and the remaining 2 Tbs. sauce.

3. Cover and microwave until the pasta is tender, about 8½ minutes.

• • • • • • • • • • • • • •

SPICY KOREAN TOFU, RICE & PEAS

This is delicious with lots of other vegetables (if you don't like peas).
Try very small raw broccoli florets, raw corn kernels, or anything else
you like.

3½ oz. extra-firm tofu, cut into 8 cubes
¼ cup cooked brown or white rice
¼ cup frozen peas
1 Tbs. Korean gochujang sauce
1 Tbs. thinly sliced trimmed scallions
1 tsp. low-sodium soy sauce

1. In a small to medium bowl, stir together all of the ingredients,
then pour into a 12-oz. mug.

2. Cover and cook until hot, about 3 minutes.

RATATOUILLE

Serve this French vegetable dish over a slice of toasted country bread, preferably topped with some crumbled goat cheese. You'll swear it had simmered for an hour or two! If you like, feel free to peel the eggplant for a softer, smoother texture. Be sure to use a high-quality balsamic vinegar—the more aged, the better.

¼ cup plus 2 Tbs. marinara sauce
¼ cup grated unpeeled zucchini (about ⅓ small zucchini)
¼ cup grated unpeeled eggplant (about ⅓ small eggplant)
1 tsp. balsamic vinegar
1 tsp. honey
1 tsp. extra-virgin olive oil
1 tsp. minced garlic
¼ tsp. herbes de Provence or dried thyme
⅛ tsp. kosher salt
3 grinds of black pepper

1. In a small bowl, stir together all of the ingredients, then pour into a 12-oz. mug.

2. Cover and microwave until the vegetables and dried herbs are very tender, 6 to 7 minutes.

• • • • • • • • • • • • • •

HOT DOG WITH BARBECUE SAUCE AND CORN

Use any type of barbecue sauce with varying levels of heat and sweetness. Try this dish over a split microwaved potato or open-face biscuit.

1 hot dog, cut into 8 slices
¼ cup barbecue sauce
¼ cup raw corn kernels

1. Mix all of the ingredients together in a 12-oz. mug.

2. Cover and cook until the corn is cooked through and the hot dog is hot, 3 to 4 minutes.

GREEK BROWN RICE SALAD WITH FETA AND BELL PEPPERS

For a variation of this warm vegetarian salad, stir in some finely chopped fresh parsley and seeded, diced tomato.

> ¾ cup cooked brown rice (short or long grain)
> ¼ cup finely chopped orange bell peppers (about ½ pepper)
> ¼ cup ⅓-inch raw broccoli florets
> 3 Tbs. crumbled feta
> ¼ tsp. lemon zest
> ⅛ tsp. kosher salt

1. Stir together all of the ingredients in a small to medium bowl, then pour into a 16-oz. mug.

2. Cover and microwave until the broccoli is tender, about 4 minutes.

• • • • • • • • • • • • • • •

MEXICAN CORN SOUP WITH BLACK BEANS

Top with finely chopped fresh cilantro leaves, salsa, or guacamole, with tortilla chips on the side. If you can't find prepared corn soup, try pumpkin or tomato.

> 1 cup canned corn soup
> ¼ cup canned salt-free black beans, rinsed and drained
> ¼ cup chopped seeded tomato (about ½ tomato)
> 2 Tbs. raw corn kernels
> 1 Tbs. thinly sliced trimmed scallions
> ¼ tsp. chili powder
> ¼ tsp. kosher salt

1. In a small to medium bowl, stir together all of the ingredients, then pour into a 16-oz. mug.

2. Cover and microwave until the corn is tender and the soup is hot, about 3 minutes.

TOMATO STUFFED WITH GOAT CHEESE AND RICE

Try variations using different types of cheese and grains. You can also swap in olive tapenade for the pesto. Garnish with fresh basil, if you like.

3 Tbs. cooked brown rice (short or long grain)
2 Tbs. goat cheese
1 Tbs. pesto
1 medium ripe tomato, stem removed
⅛ tsp. kosher salt
2 grinds of black pepper
1 Tbs. plain whole-wheat breadcrumbs
1 tsp. extra-virgin olive oil

1. Stir together the rice, cheese, and pesto in a small bowl.

2. With a small spoon or melon baller, scoop down into the whole tomato at the stem end and remove the seeds, leaving the fruit intact as best as possible. Place the tomato in a 12-oz. mug, then sprinkle it with the salt and pepper. Stuff the tomato cavity with the cheese mixture. Sprinkle with breadcrumbs and drizzle with oil.

3. Cover and microwave until the tomato is tender and the cheese melts, about 3 minutes.

HAWAIIAN-STYLE PINEAPPLE FRIED RICE

This sweet and salty rice is delicious for lunch or dinner, but it also makes a hearty breakfast meal.

½ cup cooked brown or white rice (short or long grain)
¼ cup fresh, frozen (thawed and drained) or canned and drained pineapple chunks
3 Tbs. crumbled cooked bacon (about 3 strips)
1 Tbs. thinly sliced trimmed scallions (dark green parts only)
1 Tbs. low-sodium soy sauce
1 large egg
2 grinds of black pepper

1. In a small to medium bowl, stir together the rice, pineapple, bacon, scallions, and soy sauce. Pour into a 16-oz. mug, crack the egg over the top, and sprinkle with pepper.

2. Cover and microwave until the egg white is fully cooked, about 3 minutes.

JAPANESE SMOKED SALMON WITH RICE AND AVOCADO

This dish tastes like miso soup, but richer from the salmon and avocado. You'll swear you're at the best Japanese restaurant. Feel free to crack an egg on top before microwaving the dish. For a beautiful presentation, invert onto a plate and then top with the avocado.

3½ oz. smoked salmon, coarsely chopped (about ½ cup)
¾ cup cooked white rice (ideally short grain, such as sushi)
1 Tbs. thinly sliced trimmed scallions
2 tsp. low-sodium soy sauce
2 tsp. unseasoned rice-wine vinegar
1 tsp. mirin (sweet Japanese wine) or honey
½ tsp. sesame oil
½ tsp. sesame seeds
½ avocado, diced

1. Combine the salmon, rice, scallions, soy sauce, vinegar, mirin or honey, oil, and sesame seeds in a medium bowl and stir together. Pour into a 16-oz. mug and pack down.

2. Cover and microwave until the scallions are tender, about 3 minutes. Top with the avocado.

WARM COUSCOUS SALAD WITH DRIED APRICOTS AND CHICKPEAS

Although this salad is delicious at room temperature or chilled, it's best warm because the heat helps to meld the flavors. Try it served with a dollop of plain Greek yogurt.

Heaping 1 cup cooked instant couscous (about 3 oz. dried)
¼ cup plus 2 Tbs. canned salt-free chickpeas, rinsed and drained
2 Tbs. finely chopped dried (sulfured) apricots (about 4)
2 tsp. finely chopped lightly toasted pistachios
1 Tbs. olive oil
2½ tsp. fresh lemon juice
1 tsp. finely chopped fresh flat-leaf parsley leaves
1 tsp. honey
Scant ¼ tsp. kosher salt
⅛ tsp. ground cumin
⅛ tsp. ground coriander

1. Stir together all of the ingredients in a medium bowl and pour into a 16-oz. mug.

2. Cover and microwave until the dish is hot, about 2 minutes.

DESSERT

STRAWBERRY BASIL SHORTCAKE

This springtime dessert is light and elegant. The fresh basil is a surprising addition.

1 cup ½-inch pieces fresh strawberries (4 to 5 large)
1 Tbs. honey
1 Tbs. finely chopped fresh basil leaves
1 tsp. lemon zest
⅛ tsp. kosher salt
1 cup ½-inch cubes pound cake
Vanilla ice cream, whipped topping, or homemade
    whipped cream, for serving

1. In a small to medium bowl, stir together the strawberries, honey, basil, zest, and salt until well mixed.

2. Place half of the cake in a 16-oz. mug. Top with half of the strawberry mixture, then add the remaining cake, then the remaining berry mixture. Press down firmly.

3. Cover and microwave until the cake is hot, about 2 minutes. Serve with ice cream or whipped cream.

"BAKED" APPLE WITH GRANOLA AND CINNAMON

Instead of granola, try a mixture of chopped nuts and dried fruit in this healthful dessert. This also makes a nice snack or breakfast.

Nonstick cooking spray
1 small sweet apple (that will fit inside your mug), such as a McIntosh, Rome, or Jonagold, cored with an apple corer and stem removed
1/8 tsp. ground cinnamon
1/16 tsp. kosher salt
2 Tbs. plain granola
1 Tbs. pure maple syrup
1/2 tsp. fresh lemon or apple juice
1 tsp. unsalted butter, diced
Vanilla ice cream or Greek yogurt, for serving (optional)

1. Spray the inside of a 12-oz. mug with cooking spray.

2. Place the apple in the mug and sprinkle with cinnamon and salt. Stuff the cavity with granola, and pour the syrup and lemon or apple juice on top. Sprinkle with the butter.

3. Cover and microwave until the apple is tender but still retains its shape, 1½ to 2 minutes (check after 1 minute). Top with ice cream or yogurt, if desired.

CHOCOLATE TRUFFLES WITH DRIED APRICOTS AND PISTACHIOS

These truffles are very sophisticated and not too sweet. Feel free to substitute another type of nut or dried fruit. If you prefer your truffles sweeter, you can also roll them in sweetened cocoa powder or confectioners' sugar.

> Nonstick cooking spray
> 1/4 cup semisweet chocolate chips
> 1 Tbs. finely chopped shelled pistachios
> 3 dried apricots (sulfured), finely chopped (about 1 Tbs.)
> 1/8 tsp. kosher salt
> 1 tsp. unsweetened cocoa powder

1. Spray the inside of a 12-oz. mug with cooking spray.

2. Pour the chocolate chips into the mug, cover, and microwave for about 45 seconds, until they're about 85% melted. Stir until smooth, then mix in the pistachios, apricots, and salt until combined.

3. Let cool for about 3 minutes, then when cool enough to handle, roll into three 1-inch balls. Pour the cocoa powder into a small bowl and roll the balls in it, coating them fully. Place the truffles on a small piece of waxed paper or parchment and chill until cold, 30 minutes or more.

BANANA CARAMEL PIE

This treat, inspired by banoffi pie (a British dessert), is impressive. If preparing your own whipped cream, beat chilled heavy cream on medium-high speed until soft peaks form. Use a vegetable peeler on a bar of bittersweet chocolate to make the chocolate shavings.

1 Tbs. unsalted butter
⅓ cup graham cracker crumbs
1 ripe banana, cut into ½-inch-thick slices
3 Tbs. caramel or dulce de leche sauce
¼ cup whipped topping or homemade whipped cream,
    for serving
1 tsp. chocolate shavings, for serving

1. Add the butter to a 12-oz. mug and cover. Microwave until melted, about 40 seconds.

2. Stir in the graham cracker crumbs and mix well, pressing into the bottom of the mug with the back of a spoon. Top with the bananas and caramel sauce.

3. Cover and microwave until the bananas are warm, about 1½ minutes. Top with whipped cream and chocolate.

BANANA-CHOCOLATE CHIP-COCONUT PUDDING CAKE

For a really decadent treat, invert the steamed cake onto a plate and top it with chocolate sauce; whipped topping, homemade whipped cream, or ice cream; and more shredded sweetened coconut.

Nonstick cooking spray
1 very ripe banana, mashed (½ cup)
¼ cup plus 1 Tbs. all-purpose flour
2 Tbs. chocolate chips
2 Tbs. honey
2 Tbs. coconut oil
1 large egg
1 Tbs. shredded sweetened coconut
½ tsp. baking powder
Scant ¼ tsp. kosher salt

1. Spray the inside of a 16-oz. mug with cooking spray.

2. In a small bowl, stir together all of the ingredients and pour into the mug.

3. Cover and microwave until cooked through in the center, 2½ to 3 minutes.

MOLTEN CHOCOLATE CAKE WITH TRUFFLE FILLING

This simple cake is the little black dress of mug desserts! Try it with whipped topping or homemade whipped cream, confectioners' sugar, fudge sauce, or fresh berries.

Nonstick cooking spray
3 Tbs. all-purpose flour
2 Tbs. unsweetened cocoa powder
½ tsp. baking powder
⅛ tsp. kosher salt
2 Tbs. vegetable oil
3 Tbs. honey
1 large egg
½ tsp. pure vanilla extract
1 chocolate truffle
Warm caramel or fudge sauce, fresh berries, and whipped
    topping or homemade whipped cream, for serving

1. Spray the inside of a 16-oz. mug with cooking spray.

2. Whisk together the flour, cocoa powder, baking powder, and salt in a small bowl. In another small bowl, whisk together the oil, honey, egg, and vanilla. Pour the dry mixture into the wet mixture and mix just until combined (do not overmix). Pour into the mug. Using the fork, push the truffle down into the center of the batter.

3. Cover and microwave just until the cake is cooked through but slightly molten at the bottom, 1 to 1½ minutes. (Check after 1 minute to avoid overcooking. To check, insert a sharp knife through the center of the cake until it touches the bottom of the mug—if the knife comes out wet, the center is still molten.) If desired, invert onto a plate (the top of the cake—which cooked at the bottom of the mug—should be molten) and serve with any or all of the garnishes.

APPLE CARAMEL CAKE

This tender, moist cake is delicious drizzled with extra caramel or even cider sauce.

Nonstick cooking spray
¼ cup all-purpose flour
½ tsp. baking powder
¼ tsp. ground cinnamon
⅛ tsp. kosher salt
3 Tbs. caramel sauce, plus extra for serving
2 Tbs. applesauce
2 Tbs. vegetable oil
1 large egg
¼ tsp. pure vanilla extract

1. Spray the inside of a 16-oz. mug with cooking spray.

2. In a small bowl, use a fork to whisk together the flour, baking powder, cinnamon, and salt. In another small bowl, whisk together the caramel sauce, applesauce, oil, egg, and vanilla. Add the dry mixture to the wet mixture and whisk just until combined (do not overmix). Pour into the mug.

3. Cover and microwave just until the cake is cooked through, about 2 minutes. Carefully invert onto a plate, drizzle with extra caramel sauce, and serve.

CHERRY BROWN BETTY

There's apple brown betty—and now an individual-size cherry version. You can make this dessert with virtually any fruit—fresh, frozen, or canned. If using fresh or canned, cook for less time, checking for doneness after 1 minute. If using canned, opt for a bit less sweetener as well.

1 cup frozen unsweetened cherries or other berries (not thawed)
1 Tbs. honey
1 tsp. fresh lemon juice
½ tsp. pure vanilla extract
⅛ tsp. kosher salt
⅛ tsp. ground cinnamon or nutmeg
¼ cup graham cracker crumbs
1 Tbs. unsalted butter, melted
Ice cream and chopped toasted pistachios or pecans,
    for serving (optional)

1. In a small bowl, stir together the cherries, honey, lemon juice, vanilla, salt, and cinnamon.

2. Pour into a 12-oz. mug and top with the graham cracker crumbs and melted butter.

3. Cover and microwave until hot and the cherries are tender, about 2 minutes. Top with ice cream and nuts, if desired.

CHOCOLATE FONDUE

Try this treat for Valentine's Day, a date, or even an everyday decadent reward. The recipe makes enough for one generous or two moderately sized servings. Be careful not to overcook the chocolate, as it can scorch.

¼ cup plus 2 Tbs. semisweet chocolate chips
¼ cup heavy cream
¼ tsp. pure vanilla extract
⅛ tsp. kosher salt
Pretzels, fresh fruit, pound cake cubes, or marshmallows,
    for serving

1. In a 12-oz. mug, stir together ¼ cup of the chocolate chips, the cream, vanilla, and salt.

2. Cover and microwave for about 40 seconds. Add the remaining chocolate chips, stirring until a smooth sauce forms. Serve with pretzels, fresh fruit, pound cake, or marshmallows.

• • • • • • • • • • • • •

CHOCOLATE PRETZEL BARK

Try making other types of bark—with nuts, spices, dried fruit, or chopped peppermint candies. Barks make terrific holiday gifts.

Nonstick cooking spray
¼ cup semisweet chocolate chips
1 tsp. vegetable oil
1 Tbs. plus 1 tsp. crushed pretzels

1. Spray the inside of a 12-oz. mug with cooking spray.

2. In the mug, stir together the chocolate and oil. Cover and microwave until the chocolate melts, about 1 minute (no longer, or it could scorch).

3. Pour onto a sheet of parchment and, using a spoon, spread out into an even rectangle, roughly 4 by 3 inches. Sprinkle the pretzels on top. Chill until cold (20 to 30 minutes), then peel the bark off the parchment.

BERRY SHORTCAKE WITH CRUMBLED BISCUIT

Feel free to substitute frozen berries for the fresh, but cook the shortcake for slightly more time, an extra 45 seconds (don't defrost the berries before using). If you like cinnamon, sprinkle on just a bit before serving.

Nonstick cooking spray
1 cup fresh blueberries
½ cup fresh raspberries
2 Tbs. honey
2 tsp. fresh orange juice
1 tsp. orange zest
¼ tsp. ground cinnamon, plus more for sprinkling (optional)
⅛ tsp. kosher salt
½ cup packed crumbled biscuit (about ½ biscuit)
1 Tbs. unsalted butter, melted
¼ cup vanilla ice cream, for serving (optional)

1. Spray the inside of a 16-oz. mug with cooking spray.

2. In a small bowl, mix together the blueberries, raspberries, honey, orange juice, zest, ⅛ tsp. of the cinnamon, and the salt. Pour into the mug and pack down with a spoon.

3. Top with the crumbled biscuit, then the melted butter; sprinkle with the remaining ⅛ tsp. cinnamon and pack down again.

4. Cover and microwave until the berries are tender and hot, about 2 minutes. If desired, serve with ice cream and sprinkle with cinnamon.

PEACH AND CORNBREAD SHORTCAKE

If you use fresh peaches, cook the shortcake for less time, about
2 minutes. If the fruit is tart, add a bit more preserves.

Nonstick cooking spray
1 cup frozen or fresh peach slices (not thawed if frozen)
2 Tbs. peach or apricot preserves, plus more as needed
1/8 tsp. kosher salt
1/8 tsp. ground cinnamon
1/2 cup 1-inch cubes cornbread
1 Tbs. unsalted butter, melted
1/4 cup whipped topping, homemade whipped cream, or vanilla ice
    cream, for serving (optional)

1. Spray the inside of a 12-oz. mug with cooking spray.

2. In a small bowl, mix together the peaches, preserves, salt,
and cinnamon, and pour into the mug. Pack down. Top with the
cornbread and then the melted butter.

3. Cover and cook the shortcake until the fruit is tender, about
3 minutes. If desired, top with whipped cream or ice cream.

PEANUT BUTTER AND CHOCOLATE ICE CREAM SUNDAE

Instead of the chocolate chips—and for more nutty flavor and crunch—opt for finely chopped salted peanuts. Or use both if you like! For a richer, creamier sauce, stir 2 Tbs. heavy cream into the peanut butter and honey before heating.

- 3 Tbs. creamy peanut butter
- 1 Tbs. honey
- ½ tsp. pure vanilla extract
- 2 scoops vanilla ice cream
- 1 Tbs. semisweet chocolate chips

1. In a 12-oz. mug, stir together the peanut butter, honey, and vanilla.

2. Cover and microwave until hot and smooth, 30 seconds to 1 minute (do not overcook).

3. Scoop the ice cream into a bowl, stir the sauce, then spoon it over the top. Sprinkle with the chocolate chips and serve.

PEACH MELBA

Inspired by the old-time dessert, this treat would be delicious over a slice of toasted pound cake. If using fresh peaches, remove the skin and cook for less time; start checking at 1 minute. If you use canned peaches, drain them first.

Nonstick cooking spray
8 frozen unsweetened peach slices (not thawed), cut into chunks
¼ cup raspberry dessert sauce
1 Tbs. lemon zest
1 scoop vanilla ice cream, for serving

1. Spray the inside of a 12-oz. mug with cooking spray.

2. In a small bowl, stir together the peaches, raspberry sauce, and zest. Pour into the mug.

3. Cover and microwave until the peaches are tender and warm, about 2½ minutes. Top with the ice cream.

• • • • • • • • • • • • • •

APPLE PIE NOODLE KUGEL

Traditionally made with farmer's cheese, butter, and eggs, this version of a classic Jewish side dish is much lighter. Feel free to top with a dollop of sour cream.

1 cup cooked and cooled whole-wheat fettuccini or egg noodles
¼ cup graham cracker crumbs
¼ cup raisins
¼ cup almond (or cow's) milk
¼ cup applesauce
1 Tbs. honey
1 tsp. pure vanilla extract
¼ tsp. ground cinnamon
¼ tsp. kosher salt

1. In a small bowl, stir together all of the ingredients and pour into a 12-oz. mug. Pack down.

2. Cover and cook until warm, about 1½ minutes.

WARM S'MORES DIP WITH BERRIES

Coat strawberries with this warm, candy bar–like dip. Any kids—and the kid in you—will love this!

Nonstick cooking spray
¼ cup graham cracker crumbs
2 tsp. unsalted butter, melted
2 Tbs. semisweet chocolate chips
2 Tbs. mini marshmallows
⅛ tsp. ground cinnamon
About 6 large strawberries (hulled, if desired), for dipping

1. Spray an 8-oz. mug with cooking spray.

2. Add the graham cracker crumbs and butter, mix, and pat down with a spoon. Add the chocolate chips and then the marshmallows.

3. Cover and microwave until the marshmallows and chips melt, about 1 minute (more than that and the chocolate could scorch). Sprinkle with the cinnamon and serve with the whole strawberries for dipping.

LEMON CURD CAKE

Be sure to serve this cake in the mug—it doesn't invert well. If you like, top with some whipped topping or homemade whipped cream and fresh blueberries. It's important to use a greased plate to cover the cake before cooking; otherwise, the batter can stick to the surface and not come off.

Nonstick cooking spray
¼ cup plus 1 Tbs. lemon curd
1 Tbs. vegetable oil
¼ cup all-purpose flour
¼ tsp. baking powder
¼ tsp. baking soda
⅛ tsp. kosher salt

1. Spray the inside of a 16-oz. mug with cooking spray. Spray a small plate with cooking spray.

2. In a small to medium bowl, whisk together the lemon curd and oil. In a small bowl, whisk together the flour, baking powder, baking soda, and salt until well mixed. Pour the dry ingredients into the wet and stir just until combined.

3. Scrape the batter into the greased mug. Place the greased plate over the mug with the sprayed side down (the batter is very sticky and could otherwise stick to the plate). Microwave, covered, until the cake is cooked through, about 2 minutes.

CHOCOLATE CRISPY RICE COOKIES

Here's a near-instant way to prepare a classic childhood bake sale treat, with a chocolate-y twist and a new form—cookies! Be sure to use a high-quality fudge sauce.

1 Tbs. unsalted butter
Nonstick cooking spray
¾ cup chocolate crispy rice cereal
¼ cup mini marshmallows
1 Tbs. chocolate fudge sauce

1. Place the butter in a 12-oz. mug, cover, and microwave until melted, about 40 seconds.

2. Spray the inside of the mug with cooking spray. Stir in the cereal, marshmallows, and fudge sauce, mixing well. Cover and microwave until the marshmallows have fully melted, about 1 minute (check after 40 seconds).

3. Divide into two piles on a piece of waxed paper or parchment. Form into 2-inch-diameter "cookie" shapes and refrigerate until cool and solid, about 30 minutes.

DOUBLE CHOCOLATE CAKE WITH DRIED CRANBERRIES

This cake is just as delicious with sweetened dried cherries or shredded sweetened coconut in place of the cranberries.

Nonstick cooking spray
3 Tbs. all-purpose flour
1 Tbs. unsweetened cocoa powder
½ tsp. baking powder
⅛ tsp. kosher salt
2 Tbs. plus 1 tsp. fudge sauce
3 Tbs. vegetable oil
1 large egg
¼ tsp. pure vanilla extract
2 Tbs. chocolate chips (I like semisweet,
   but dark or milk would also work well)
2 Tbs. dried cranberries
1 scoop vanilla ice cream, for serving

1. Spray the inside of a 12-oz. mug with cooking spray.

2. In a small bowl, use a fork to whisk together the flour, cocoa powder, baking powder, and salt. In another small bowl, stir together 2 Tbs. of the fudge sauce, the oil, egg, and vanilla, and whisk until mixed. Add the dry mixture to the wet mixture and stir together just until mixed (do not overmix). Stir in the chocolate chips and cranberries and pour into the greased mug.

3. Cover and microwave just until the cake is cooked through, about 2 minutes. Serve right in the mug, topped with ice cream and the remaining fudge sauce, or invert the cake onto a plate and then add the toppings.

WHITE CHOCOLATE FONDUE

Serve this creamy dessert sauce with fresh strawberries or other fruit.

> ¼ cup white chocolate chips
> 2 tsp. heavy cream
> ⅛ tsp. kosher salt
> Fresh fruit, such as strawberries, for serving

1. Stir together the white chocolate chips, cream, and salt in a 12-oz. mug.

2. Cover and microwave until the chips are almost melted, about 30 seconds. Stir well. Some of the fat will have separated out; stir it back in until you achieve a smooth, creamy consistency. Serve immediately with fresh fruit.

• • • • • • • • • • • • • •

STRAWBERRY RICE PUDDING

Here's a resourceful way to use extra cooked rice. In addition to dessert, the rice pudding makes a decadent breakfast.

> ¾ cup cooked white rice (preferably short grain)
> ½ cup milk
> ½ cup chopped fresh strawberries (about 3 large)
> ¼ cup strawberry preserves
> ½ tsp. pure vanilla extract
> ¼ tsp. ground cinnamon
> ⅛ tsp. kosher salt

1. Mix together all of the ingredients in a small to medium bowl and pour into a 16-oz. mug.

2. Cover and microwave until warm and creamy, about 4 minutes.

BLACK FOREST CAKE WITH CHERRY PRESERVES AND COCONUT

Cherry preserves and sweetened shredded coconut take this rich chocolate cake over the top. Try varying the recipe with another type of preserves, such as orange marmalade, and nuts instead of the coconut.

Nonstick cooking spray
3 Tbs. all-purpose flour
3 Tbs. granulated sugar
2 Tbs. unsweetened cocoa powder
½ tsp. baking powder
⅛ tsp. kosher salt
3 Tbs. vegetable oil
1 large egg
1 Tbs. cherry or raspberry preserves
1 Tbs. sweetened shredded coconut

1. Spray the inside of a 16-oz. mug with cooking spray.

2. In a small bowl, use a fork to whisk together the flour, sugar, cocoa powder, baking powder, and salt until thoroughly mixed. In another small bowl, whisk together the oil and egg until smooth. Pour the oil-egg mixture into the dry mixture and mix just until thoroughly blended (do not overmix). Pour into the mug and top with the preserves and coconut.

3. Cover and microwave until just cooked through in the center, about 90 seconds (do not overcook).

WARM CHERRY ALMOND POUND CAKE

When they're in season, use fresh cherries in this yummy cake. For variation, try vanilla extract instead of almond extract and top with some finely chopped pistachios rather than almonds.

1 cup frozen dark sweet cherries
1 Tbs. honey
½ tsp. almond extract
½ tsp. fresh lemon juice
⅛ tsp. ground cinnamon
⅛ tsp. kosher salt
1 cup ½-inch cubes pound cake
Whipped topping, homemade whipped cream, or vanilla ice cream, for serving (optional)
1 tsp. finely chopped toasted almonds, for serving (optional)

1. In a small to medium bowl, gently stir together all of the ingredients except for the optional toppings. Pour into a 16-oz. mug, scraping out any remaining honey from the bowl. Use your spoon to press the dessert down into the mug.

2. Cover and microwave until the dessert is hot, about 3 minutes. Top with whipped cream and nuts, if you like, and serve.

PUMPKIN CAKE WITH COCONUT AND LIME

Moist and tropical, this cake is especially unique. Serve it in the mug, topped with a scoop of ice cream. The cake has a tendency to overflow in the microwave, so cover tightly to keep your microwave clean!

    Nonstick cooking spray
    ½ cup all-purpose flour
    ½ tsp. baking powder
    ¼ tsp. baking soda
    ¼ tsp. kosher salt
    ¼ cup plus 2 Tbs. canned pumpkin or butternut squash purée
    3 Tbs. canned coconut milk (full fat), well shaken
    2 Tbs. maple syrup
    2 Tbs. vegetable oil
    1 large egg
    ¼ tsp. lime zest

1. Spray a 16-oz. mug with cooking spray.

2. In a small bowl, whisk together the flour, baking powder, baking soda, and salt until well mixed. In a medium bowl, whisk together the pumpkin, coconut milk, maple syrup, oil, egg, and zest until well mixed. Add the dry mixture to the wet mixture and stir just until combined. Pour into the greased mug.

3. Cover tightly and microwave until the center is cooked through, 2 to 2½ minutes.

HOT PEACH AND CINNAMON RAISIN BREAD PUDDING

If you can't find a canister-shaped loaf of cinnamon raisin bread, use 3 slices from a rectangular loaf and cut into rounds slightly smaller than the diameter of your mug.

- **1 cup frozen peach chunks (not thawed)**
- **1 Tbs. granulated sugar**
- **1 tsp. lemon zest**
- **½ tsp. fresh lemon juice**
- **⅛ tsp. ground cinnamon**
- **⅛ tsp. kosher salt**
- **¼ cup milk**
- **3 thin round slices cinnamon raisin bread**
- **Vanilla ice cream, for serving (optional)**

1. In a small to medium bowl, mix together the peaches, sugar, lemon zest and juice, cinnamon, and salt.

2. Pour the milk into a shallow bowl. Dip both sides of 1 bread slice into the milk and fit it into the bottom of the mug. Spoon one-third of the peach mixture on top of the bread in the mug. Repeat layering with the remaining 2 slices of bread and remaining two-thirds of the peach mixture, ending with the peach mixture.

3. Cover and microwave until the dessert is fully hot, about 3 minutes. Top with ice cream, if you like.

CLASSIC RICE PUDDING WITH CINNAMON AND RAISINS

Serve warm or cold, sprinkled with a pinch more cinnamon. If serving cold, stir in some whipped topping to make the rice pudding even richer and creamier.

> 1 cup cooked white rice (short or long grain)
> ½ cup milk
> 2 Tbs. raisins
> 1 Tbs. plus 1 tsp. granulated sugar
> ½ tsp. pure vanilla extract
> ½ tsp. cornstarch
> ¼ tsp. ground cinnamon
> ⅛ tsp. kosher salt

1. Stir together all of the ingredients in a small to medium bowl.

2. Pour into a 12-oz. mug, cover, and microwave until hot and creamy, about 2 minutes.

• • • • • • • • • • • • • •

COCONUT RICE PUDDING WITH INDIAN SPICES

Serve warm or cold, sprinkled with finely chopped toasted pistachios, more golden raisins, or more cardamom.

> 1 cup cooked white rice (short or long grain)
> ½ cup canned coconut milk (full fat), well shaken
> 2 Tbs. golden raisins
> 1 Tbs. plus 2 tsp. granulated sugar
> ½ tsp. cornstarch
> ¼ tsp. rosewater
> ¼ tsp. ground cardamom
> ⅛ tsp. kosher salt

1. Stir together all of the ingredients in a small to medium bowl.

2. Pour into a 12-oz. mug, cover, and microwave until hot and creamy, about 2 minutes.

COCONUT SNOWBALL TRUFFLES

These truffles would make an ideal winter holiday gift. If you don't like ginger, try golden raisins or finely chopped dried apricots.

Nonstick cooking spray
¼ cup white chocolate chips
1 Tbs. shredded unsweetened coconut
1 tsp. minced crystallized ginger
⅛ tsp. kosher salt

1. Spray the inside of a 12-oz. mug with cooking spray.

2. Pour the white chocolate chips into the mug, cover, and microwave for about 45 seconds, until they're about 85% melted. Stir until smooth. Add 1 tsp. of the coconut, the ginger, and the salt, and stir until well mixed.

3. Let cool for about 3 minutes, then when cool enough to handle, roll into two 1-inch balls. Pour the remaining coconut into a small bowl and roll the balls in it, coating them fully. Place the truffles on a small piece of waxed paper or parchment and chill until cold, 30 minutes or more.

TRES LECHES CAKE

Meaning "three milks," this Mexican cake is traditionally made with sweetened condensed milk, regular milk, and cream. Here, I've substituted coconut milk for the cream. Since sweetened condensed milk is so, well, sweet, no additional sweetener is needed. The ultimate in comfort food, this treat is best eaten straight out of the mug.

¼ cup sweetened condensed milk
¼ cup milk
¼ cup canned coconut milk (full fat), well shaken
½ tsp. cornstarch
½ tsp. pure vanilla extract
⅛ tsp. kosher salt
1 cup packed 1-inch cubes pound cake (about 2 slices)

1. In a small to medium bowl, stir together the three milks, cornstarch, vanilla, and salt until well mixed.

2. Place half of the cake cubes on the bottom of a 12-oz. mug. Pour half of the milk mixture on top. Repeat with the remaining cake cubes and milk mixture, pressing them down.

3. Cover and microwave until hot, about 2 minutes.

CHOCOLATE ESPRESSO PUDDING WITH ORANGE

The orange adds a tart, fruity note to this sophisticated, not-too-sweet dessert.

> **2 Tbs. light brown sugar**
> **1½ Tbs. unsweetened cocoa powder**
> **2 tsp. cornstarch**
> **1 tsp. espresso powder**
> **½ tsp. orange zest**
> **⅛ tsp. ground cinnamon**
> **⅛ tsp. kosher salt**
> **½ cup milk**
> **½ tsp. pure vanilla extract**
> **Whipped topping or homemade whipped cream, for serving**

1. In a small bowl, whisk together the brown sugar, cocoa powder, cornstarch, espresso powder, zest, ground cinnamon, and salt. Add the milk and vanilla and whisk until no lumps remain. Pour into a 16-oz. mug.

2. Cover and microwave until the pudding is relatively thick and smooth, about 3 minutes.

3. Pour into a smaller (8-oz.) serving mug or cup and let cool for 10 minutes. Place a piece of plastic wrap directly on the surface and transfer to the fridge to chill until cold, about 2 hours. Top with whipped cream.

MANGO COCONUT CRUMBLE

If you like, vary this tropical dessert by using fresh or canned and drained pineapple chunks instead of the mango. Omit the ginger if you don't like it.

¾ cup frozen mango chunks (not thawed)
2 Tbs. maple syrup
1 tsp. fresh lime juice
1 tsp. all-purpose flour
½ tsp. minced crystallized ginger
¼ tsp. ground cinnamon
⅛ tsp. kosher salt
2 Tbs. shredded sweetened coconut
2 Tbs. plain granola
1 tsp. unsalted butter, melted
Scoop of ice cream, sorbet, or Greek yogurt, for serving
(tropical or plain flavor—your choice!)

1. In a small bowl, stir together the mango chunks, syrup, lime juice, flour, ginger, half of the cinnamon, and the salt. Pour into a 12-oz. mug and sprinkle with the coconut, granola, remaining cinnamon, and melted butter.

2. Cover and microwave until hot and the fruit filling cooks through, about 2½ minutes. Top with ice cream, sorbet, or yogurt.

CLASSIC GINGERBREAD

Applesauce adds moisture without extra fat. Try garnishing this cake—large enough for two servings—with vanilla ice cream, whipped topping, or homemade whipped cream.

Nonstick cooking spray
½ cup all-purpose flour
1 Tbs. light brown sugar
½ tsp. baking soda
½ tsp. orange zest
¼ tsp. ground ginger
⅛ tsp. ground cloves
⅛ tsp. ground cinnamon
⅛ tsp. kosher salt
3 Tbs. applesauce
3 Tbs. vegetable oil
1 large egg
1 Tbs. plus 1 tsp. molasses

1. Spray the inside of a 16-oz. mug with cooking spray.

2. In a small bowl, use a fork to whisk together the flour, brown sugar, baking soda, zest, ginger, cloves, cinnamon, and salt. In another small to medium bowl, whisk together the applesauce, oil, egg, and molasses. Pour the dry ingredients into the wet and mix just until combined. Pour into the mug and cover.

3. Microwave until just cooked through in the center, about 2 minutes (do not overcook).

WARM GUAVA SAUCE OVER TOASTED POUND CAKE

Guava paste can be found in the Mexican/Latin American section of most grocery stores (look for the Goya® products). Top this decadent dessert with a scoop of vanilla or cinnamon ice cream. The recipe makes enough sauce for one large portion or two more moderate portions (if making two servings, you might want to toast another slice of pound cake). Wait for a few minutes after preparing the sauce to serve—it comes out of the microwave very hot.

Nonstick cooking spray
3½ oz. guava paste (about ½ cup, cubed)
2 Tbs. fresh orange juice
1 slice pound cake, toasted

1. Spray the inside of a 12-oz. mug with cooking spray.

2. Add the guava paste and orange juice to the mug, cover, and microwave until most of the paste melts, about 1 minute. Stir well, until smooth.

3. Place the toasted pound cake on a plate and pour the guava sauce over the top.

NUTELLA CAKE ▶

Brownie-like, this cake lets the richness and flavor of everyone's favorite chocolate-hazelnut spread shine. When inverted, the dessert has a slightly molten top.

> **Nonstick cooking spray**
> **¼ cup all-purpose flour**
> **½ tsp. baking powder**
> **⅛ tsp. kosher salt**
> **½ cup Nutella® (or other chocolate-hazelnut spread)**
> **1 large egg**

1. Spray the inside of a 16-oz. mug with cooking spray.

2. In a small bowl, whisk together the flour, baking powder, and salt until fully combined. In a medium bowl, whisk together the Nutella and egg until well mixed. Add the dry mixture to the wet mixture and stir until fully combined. Pour into the greased mug.

3. Cover tightly and microwave until the bottom is 90% cooked through, about 2 minutes. If desired, invert onto a dessert plate.

• • • • • • • • • • • • • •

WARM MANGO-LIME SOUP

Top this dessert soup with any of the following for a full yum factor: a scoop of coconut sorbet or gelato, sweetened shredded coconut, fresh mango chunks, or fresh raspberries. Since the mango and juice are sweet, you shouldn't need any sweetener, but if you'd like a little boost, feel free to stir in some honey or agave nectar.

> **¾ cup mango juice**
> **½ cup frozen mango chunks (not thawed)**
> **¼ tsp. lime zest**

1. Stir together the ingredients in a 16-oz. mug.

2. Cover and microwave until hot, about 3 minutes.

WARM COCONUT LIME TRIFLE

Reserve the pineapple juice for another use, such as a tropical drink. For an elegant presentation, garnish with lime zest. Be sure to use soft, not crispy, ladyfingers, as you would for tiramisu.

Nonstick cooking spray
¼ cup sweetened condensed milk
½ cup canned coconut milk (full fat), well shaken
2 tsp. fresh lime juice
½ tsp. cornstarch
6 soft ladyfinger cookies
One 8-oz. can crushed pineapple (about ½ cup), drained

1. Spray the inside of a 16-oz. mug with cooking spray.

2. In a small bowl, whisk together the condensed milk, half of the coconut milk, the lime juice, and cornstarch until smooth. Pour the remaining coconut milk into a shallow bowl.

3. Dip both sides of 3 cookies into the coconut milk in the shallow bowl and break in half. Fit into the bottom of the mug. Top with half of the pineapple and half of the condensed milk mixture. Dip both sides of the remaining 3 cookies into the coconut milk and break in half. Fit into the mug. Top with the remaining pineapple and condensed milk mixture, pushing down on the contents.

4. Cover and microwave until the custard on top solidifies, about 2 minutes.

WARM CHERRY-POMEGRANATE SOUP

This unusual and healthful dessert soup is delicious topped with a dollop of vanilla Greek yogurt or ice cream—it melts a bit into the soup, making it creamy. If you'd prefer the soup sweeter, add a bit more honey.

1 cup fresh or frozen dark sweet cherries (not thawed if frozen)
¾ cup unsweetened pomegranate juice
1 tsp. honey
¼ tsp. pure vanilla extract
1 cinnamon stick

1. In a small to medium bowl, stir together all of the ingredients until well mixed, then pour into a 16-oz. mug.

2. Cover and microwave until hot, about 3 minutes. Remove the cinnamon stick before eating.

• • • • • • • • • • • • • •

LIME PIE RICE PUDDING

This tropical dessert is just like key lime pie but with coconut milk. Plus it's much simpler to make!

¾ cup cooked white or brown rice (short or long grain)
½ cup canned light coconut milk, well shaken
¼ cup sweetened condensed milk
2 tsp. lime zest
1 tsp. fresh lime juice
⅛ tsp. kosher salt

1. Stir together all of the ingredients in a small bowl and pour into a 16-oz. mug.

2. Cover and microwave until hot and creamy, about 3 minutes.

ORANGE MARMALADE SPONGE CAKE

This gorgeous cake would be ideal crowned with whipped topping or homemade whipped cream. Add a dollop of marmalade, too; warm slightly and drizzle over the top.

Nonstick cooking spray
1 large egg
3 Tbs. honey
3 Tbs. vegetable oil
½ tsp. orange zest
¼ cup all-purpose flour
¼ tsp. baking soda
¼ tsp. baking powder
⅛ tsp. kosher salt
1 Tbs. orange marmalade, plus more if desired

1. Spray the inside of a 16-oz. mug with cooking spray.

2. In a small to medium bowl, whisk together the egg, honey, oil, and zest until smooth. In another small bowl, whisk together the flour, baking soda, baking powder, and salt. Mix the dry ingredients into the wet ingredients and stir until smooth. Spoon the marmalade into the mug, pour the batter on top.

3. Cover and microwave until the cake is cooked through, about 2 minutes. Carefully invert onto a plate so the marmalade side is facing up. If desired, drizzle with more marmalade.

LIQUID/DRY MEASURES

U.S.	METRIC
¼ teaspoon	1.25 milliliters
½ teaspoon	2.5 milliliters
1 teaspoon	5 milliliters
1 tablespoon (3 teaspoons)	15 milliliters
1 fluid ounce (2 tablespoons)	30 milliliters
¼ cup	60 milliliters
⅓ cup	80 milliliters
½ cup	120 milliliters
1 cup	240 milliliters
1 pint (2 cups)	480 milliliters
1 quart (4 cups; 32 ounces)	960 milliliters
1 gallon (4 quarts)	3.84 liters
1 ounce (by weight)	28 grams
1 pound	454 grams
2.2 pounds	1 kilogram

OVEN TEMPERATURES

°F	GAS MARK	°C
250	½	120
275	1	140
300	2	150
325	3	165
350	4	180
375	5	190
400	6	200
425	7	220
450	8	230
475	9	240
500	10	260
550	Broil	290

INDEX

If you like this book, you'll love *Fine Cooking.*

Read *Fine Cooking* **Magazine:**

Get six idea-filled issues including FREE tablet editions. Every issue is packed with triple-tested recipes, expert advice, step-by-step techniques – everything for people who love to cook!

Subscribe today at:
FineCooking.com/4Sub

Discover our *Fine Cooking* **Online Store:**

It's your destination for premium resources from America's best cookbook writers, chefs, and bakers: cookbooks, DVDs, videos, special interest publications, and more.

Visit today at:
FineCooking.com/4More

Get our FREE *Fine Cooking* **eNewsletter:**

Our *Fine Cooking* weekly eletter is packed with FREE recipes, chefs' tips and advice, seasonal menus, holiday inspiration, and so much more from the editors of *Fine Cooking* magazine.

Sign up, it's free:
FineCooking.com/4Newsletter

Visit our *Fine Cooking* **Website:**

Always fresh and delicious, it's where you'll find inspiration, how-to help, seasonal recipes, menus, videos, slideshows, interactive tools, our popular recipe-maker, and more.

Find more info online:
FineCooking.com/4Web

The Taunton Press

© 2014 The Taunton Press